1000 Best eBay Success Secrets

GREG HOLDEN

SOURCEBOOKS, INC.
NAPERVILLE, ILLINOIS

Published by Sourcebooks, Inc.
P.O. Box 4410, Naperville, Illinois 60567-4410
(630) 961-3900
Fax: (630) 961-2168
www.sourcebooks.com
Library of Congress Cataloging-in-Publication Data

Holden, Greg.
1000 best eBay success secrets / Greg Holden.
    p. cm.
Includes index.
ISBN-13: 978-1-4022-0805-8
ISBN-10: 1-4022-0805-7
1. eBay (Firm) 2. Internet auctions. I. Title. II. Title: One thousand best eBay success secrets.

HF5478.H644 2006
658.8'7--dc22

2006020834
Printed and bound in Canada.
WC 10 9 8 7 6 5 4 3 2

Dedication
To the members of the eBay community, who have never failed to give me a boost when I needed it and a helping hand when I asked for it.

Acknowledgments

It might look like everything in this book came from me alone. Indeed, nearly all of these tips came out of what I have learned by selling on eBay. But I could never have started the project in the first place, much less have seen it through to fruition, on my own. I owe a tremendous debt of gratitude to a multitude of people, including my agent Lynn Haller of Studio B, who has guided me to a variety of new opportunities in the past few years; Bethany Brown of Sourcebooks for being very easy to work with; my assistant Ann Lindner; and my eBay friend and mentor Paula Amato, who has helped me learn by doing.

Contents

Part One:

Before the Sale

Part One:

Before the Sale

1.

Deciding What to Sell on eBay

It's a question I hear all the time from prospective eBay sellers: "What's the best thing I can sell on eBay?" There's no simple answer—the list of desirable items changes with the seasons and as collecting fads come and go. The choice of what to sell is important, however. Take the time to choose items that you'll enjoy selling and handling for the long term. Researching merchandise, finding valuable and productive product lines, and knowing the value of what you want to sell is an ongoing process. If you play your cards right and pick products you enjoy finding and selling, you'll have taken a big first step toward becoming a successful eBay seller.

1. Sell something you love. If you have a passion for something, you won't mind the long hours you spend sourcing it. Often you'd be looking at trade magazines and browsing the Web for your field of interest anyhow, so why not have your cake and eat it too by getting paid for having fun?

2. If you're already familiar with brand names and model numbers from your collecting or hobbies, you'll find it easy to extend your knowledge into selling on eBay. It will be easier to write descriptions if you really know your topic. Plus, you can tell from a glance at a garage sale or resale shop if an object is something you're likely to be able to resell at a profit.

3. Start with some housecleaning and see what types of items interest you. Many sellers discover that one item sells for a surprisingly high amount: that old purse in the back of a closet fetches $50, or that bottle of perfume from the 1960s sells for $75. That first sale can turn into a hobby or a sales routine: if you sell one purse, you can sell more. If nothing else, you'll reduce your clutter!

4. Follow the classic route to becoming a seller on eBay. First, clean out your closet and garage and discover what you like selling. Next, scrounge around with family and friends for more merchandise, and realize you can sell just about anything. Then, scour flea markets and garage sales for more items to sell. You'll eventually find a wholesale supplier and sell regularly on the site.

5. Do you already have a business? Think about expanding to eBay. It's perfect for unloading returned merchandise or overstock you need to clear out. Like many businesspeople, you might find that the online part of your business could become more profitable than your brick-and-mortar component. The two can complement one another.

6. Don't try to sell too many different things. Stick to one or two categories that you love rather than six or seven in which you're mildly interested. You need to become an expert in at least one field so you can make wise purchases and price merchandise sensibly. Limiting your options makes it easier for you to gain the knowledge you need.

7. Assemble a team of pickers and searchers who will scour your neighborhood for the kinds of items you want to sell. Create a sales booklet with a list of brands and model numbers as well as photos of what your pickers should look for.

8. Conventional wisdom holds that if you make a steady income selling on eBay, you need to find a wholesale supplier and sell new merchandise you buy inexpensively. That's a good approach, and you can explore it more in chapter 2, but there's always a market for one-of-a-kind collectibles. It depends on what you can find. If you can find rare collectibles or hard-to-find secondhand items easily, go for it!

9. Don't get stuck in a rut with only one product line. Be open to new products and categories that are very different. One PowerSeller I know started out selling Italian charms and branched out to, of all things, home pregnancy tests and condoms. Another sells high-end fountain pens as well as men's socks and underwear.

10. Think small. The smaller your merchandise, the easier it will be to transport and sell, and the less expensive it will be to ship. If you sell things like clothing or hardware, you may end up having to find warehouse space. Items like postcards or golf balls can be stored in a more compact space and don't need to be packed so carefully for shipping.

MARKET RESEARCH

11. eBay's Completed Items search is the obvious place to start to search for merchandise that's in demand. But don't overlook eBay's Hot Items reports and specialized services like Terapeak (www.terapeak.com) which provide detailed records on completed eBay sales.

12. You don't have to invent your product line from scratch. Research sellers such as drop-off stores—stores set up especially to sell merchandise on eBay on behalf of their owners— to see what kinds of things they like to sell. Make note of the things that attract the best prices and the highest number of bids, and try to find those items yourself.

13. Research brands in your chosen field by looking through catalogs and browsing brick-and-mortar stores. I remember window shopping in Georgetown and writing down the name of an ultra-expensive shoe brand I had never heard of before: Taryn Rose. When I found a pair of used Taryn Rose slippers for $2, I snapped them up and resold them on eBay for $132.

14. When it comes to figuring out what you want to sell on eBay, think like your customers. Put yourself in their shoes. Browse through the categories in which you want to sell. Read lots of descriptions. Get a feel for which items are most desirable and attract lots of bids.

15. Give yourself a week or two, rather than an hour or two, to become an expert in your area of interest. I had someone tell me he researched eBay for three weeks before deciding to sell high-end fountain pens; he's now a PowerSeller and makes a full-time living on eBay.

16. As you do your research, think ahead to the descriptions you'll write. When you read other sales descriptions in online catalogs or on eBay, write down some ideas for keywords and phrases that might get shoppers' attention.

17. Keep researching completed auctions on eBay every couple of weeks, if not more frequently. eBay only keeps records of completed sales online for about two or three weeks. Compile a database of sales that attracted lots of bids or high prices (or both). Write down the starting bid, the number of bids, the high bid, and whether the sale ended with a Buy It Now or an auction purchase. After a few months, you'll have a database of transaction details you can refer to when you are deciding what to buy or how to price merchandise.

EVALUATING WHAT YOU HAVE TO SELL

18. After you have been selling for a while, you realize that "Like New" or "New" items tend to get the most attention, no matter what they are. Look for items in their original boxes or wrappers, or with their original price tags. These features alone will gain interest for these items on eBay.

19. Plenty of businesses offer their services as appraisers. You can even get an appraisal online: you can send in photos of your merchandise, pay a fee, and get back a detailed report on the item's value. Only use these services if you have a work of art, a rare vase or lamp, or other collectible that you suspect is really valuable. Otherwise, take advantage of eBay itself and do your own research.

20. For some highly collectible items like coins, stamps, and baseball cards, it's important to get an authentication service to grade the item's condition and certify its authenticity. For coins, check out the Professional Coin Grading Service (www.pcgs.com); for comic books, try Comics Guaranty, LLC (www.cgccomics.com).

21. You can also find grading services and professional associations related to collectibles on the category opening page on eBay. A category opening page is a sort of "welcome page" for one of eBay's top-level categories. These are the categories you see listed on the left-hand column of eBay's home page (www.ebay.com). For example, the Stamps opening page (stamps.ebay.com) has links to dealers' associations and guidelines for selling stamps.

FOCUSING YOUR SEARCHES

22. Don't focus solely on the U.S. version of eBay when you're researching items to sell. Remember that there are many separate eBay sites around the world. If you speak a foreign language, you have an advantage over other sellers: you can place ads on a foreign site. Even if you don't, you can do a search on the English-speaking versions of eBay around the world, such as eBay UK (www.ebay.co.uk), eBay Australia (www.ebay.com.au), or eBay Canada (www.ebay.ca).

23. If you shop for merchandise in your local area (at flea markets, secondhand stores, or garage sales), find out who your competition is. Do a search of completed sales for items that are similar to the ones you have to sell. Before you click the Search button, though, scroll down the Advanced Search page to the section labeled Items Near Me. Check the Items within . . . box, choose a distance (200 miles or less), and enter your zip code or city. Then click Search. This limits results to transactions of items located near your own home.

24. Once you've gathered some names of competitors in your area of interest, save their User IDs in the Favorites section of My eBay. That way, you'll be able to revisit them regularly to see what they have for sale and how many sales they have completed recently.

25. Once you've conducted a search with a complex set of variables such as location, currency, and so on, you can save your search to the My Favorite Searches area of My eBay. That way, you don't have to re-enter the search criteria every time you want to do some research. First, conduct the search. Then click the link Add to My Favorite Searches that appears at the top of the search results.

26. One of the worst places to look for merchandise you can sell on eBay is eBay itself. Yes, you occasionally find great bargains on eBay, but it's rare for sellers to be able to buy something on the auction site and then turn around and sell it for a profit. This even applies if you are considering making bulk purchases in the Wholesale Lots area of eBay (pages.ebay.com/catindex/catwholesale.html).

27. Buy out of season. Look for Christmas items in late December and January when they're on sale; store them until November or so, when you can sell them at a profit. Try to buy back-to-school clothing and supplies in early summer so you can sell them in the fall. Be patient and wait until a few weeks before the holiday or event, and then sell what you've been saving.

LOOKING CLOSE TO HOME

28. Suppose you have a successful traditional business in a brick-and-mortar store, a wholesale outlet, or another arrangement (you sell collectibles at trade shows and flea markets, for instance). You can use eBay to grow and expand your existing customer base.

29. Think of eBay as a way to acquire new business. Send an announcement to your existing customer base. Encourage your brick-and-mortar customers to visit your eBay Store, and offer them discounts if they make purchases there.

30. Make friends with the management of your local thrift store or resale shop. Let them know what you sell on eBay. You might get to see merchandise before it gets put out on the shelves, which gives you an obvious advantage over other sellers.

31. Do you have a friend or relative who is in business already and who can function as your business "coach"? Many of the most successful eBay PowerSellers started out with a helping hand from an uncle who was a wholesaler, an in-law who already sold online, or another family member. Ask around. At the very least, you'll get some good suggestions to help you get your enterprise off the ground.

32. You've probably heard the phrases "garbage picking" or "dumpster diving." These activities are not for everybody. However, if you are the sort who enjoys walking down alleys and scouring discarded items for hidden treasures, it can occasionally be a source of merchandise to sell on eBay, as long as it's in good condition. For instance, I found a pair of expensive French shoes being thrown out that I sold for more than $50. I also found college calculus textbooks in someone's garbage that I resold on eBay.

SUREFIRE MERCHANDISE TO SELL ON EBAY

33. There's one thing that nearly every family with school-age children literally has lying around and that is in high demand on eBay: textbooks. High school, college, graduate school, and test-preparation textbooks are often ridiculously expensive, and people shop for them eagerly on eBay. Ask your family and friends; they just might give you some unneeded books to sell.

34. Even if you do "garbage pick" something for resale on eBay, don't tell people that it came from the garbage. They don't need to know. And don't sell yourself short by underpricing it just because it cost you nothing. Research the item like anything else and settle on a reasonable starting bid.

35. When in doubt, $9.99 is a good starting bid for eBay. The listing fee eBay charges you for putting an item up for sale changes at $10. At this writing, the insertion fee for $9.99 is 35 cents. From $10 up to $24.99 it is 60 cents. That's a substantial jump if you're selling dozens or hundreds of items at a time.

36. Art is a notoriously difficult thing to sell on eBay. Everyone dreams of finding an original painting by a desirable artist of the sort that often turns up on *Antiques Roadshow*. But eBay is generally not the best place to get top dollar. Get a professional appraisal, and sell the artworks at an art auction, where you're more likely to get good prices.

37. There's nothing wrong with selling used merchandise. Try to find brands that attract good prices even if they are used. In the world of shoes I "walk" in, brands like Gucci and Bruno Magli are surefire sellers. Many brands of golf clubs sell well even if they're secondhand, too. Focus on quality and well-established brands and you'll find success.

38. If you're looking for a snapshot of the items that are currently hot, go to eBay Pulse (www.ebay.com/pulse). You'll find the largest eBay Stores in the category, along with the most watched items and popular keywords used in searches. Don't stick with the first Pulse page. Browse for your own category, and you'll get some revealing results.

39. Do you have products or materials on hand already that you can reuse or "repurpose"? Think creatively, and you may find a source of merchandise right at hand. Jeff McCullough, who runs a printing company called Suburban Paper Products, was walking by his garbage dumpster and noticed all the leftover colorful scraps of paper that were being thrown out after printing jobs. He decided to reuse the scraps of paper by packing them into bundles—just in time to sell them profitably on eBay during the scrapbooking craze of the late 1990s.

40. Paper items of any sort make excellent products to sell on eBay. Consider postcards, comic books, magazines, posters, or newspapers. They're lightweight, easy to pack, and you don't have to take lots of photos to depict them. In contrast, items like furniture or motor vehicles require lots of different digital images and aren't at all easy to ship.

41. Anything that runs on electricity, works, and is in good condition can be put up for sale on eBay. If you have sources for camera equipment, audio entertainment, computers, or other gadgets, go for them: they're among the best things you can sell on the auction site, despite the high number of sellers who already operate in this field.

42. eBay started as a place to buy and sell collectibles. A rare Rolls Royce Silver Shadow automobile was one of the first things that ever sold on the site. The story goes that founder Pierre Omidyar created AuctionWeb (he later changed the name to eBay) as a place to trade Pez dispensers. The point is that toys and collectibles are among the biggest sellers on eBay. If you already sell collectibles or want to, you should definitely give eBay a try.

43. Sports equipment is expensive. If you love a particular sport and you can get your hands on secondhand or wholesale equipment, turn around and sell it on the auction site.

44. There's an entire site within eBay that's devoted to buying and selling automobiles, auto parts, motorcycles, and anything that runs on an engine. It's called eBay Motors, and it's an efficient and cost-effective way to sell vehicles. Accessories like repair manuals and parts are in demand, too.

45. Chances are you don't think about eBay as a place to sell real estate, but if you're looking to open up your property to a nationwide—or more accurately, worldwide—marketplace, consider listing in eBay's Real Estate category. You don't have to think about selling your house, necessarily; the real estate category is used for advertising land, time-shares, vacation homes, and more.

46. Whatever you decide to sell on eBay, make sure you actually have the object in your hands when you start the listing. If you have the object itself but not the box, and it says you have the box in your description, don't list the item until you actually have the box, too. Why? Buyers are in a hurry. Many of them pay as soon as the sale ends with PayPal. They want you to ship as soon as possible. Don't keep them waiting, or you risk receiving negative feedback.

FINDING MERCHANDISE FOR SPECIAL TYPES OF EBAY SALES

47. If you have used books on hand that aren't necessarily textbooks and that are simply crowding your shelves (and who doesn't?), consider putting them up for sale on Half.com. Half.com is a part of eBay devoted to selling books, CDs, DVDs, and other household items. Half.com is great for beginning sellers because it's especially easy to put items online: you don't have to take photos; you don't have to write descriptions; you just set your price and indicate the condition. Find out more at half.ebay.com.

48. Do you have tickets to a concert or play and you suddenly can't use them? You can donate them back to the theater for a tax deduction. If you have a few days before the event, you can also put them up for sale on eBay. Tickets to ultra-popular Broadway shows are always in demand. The one-day auction option is frequently used by sellers who need to unload tickets in a hurry.

49. If you have X-rated videos or adult "toys" for sale, you have to list them in a special category called Adults Only. Items listed in Adults Only don't show up in regular eBay searches. Anyone who places a bid in this category has to have a credit card on file to verify his or her identity.

50. Suppose you want to sell something to buyers who want to keep their identities private for one reason or another. You can hold a Private Auction. In this type of eBay sale, bidders' names are kept secret and not revealed on the auction site.

2.

Wholesale Suppliers and Other Sourcing Resources

If you only want to sell on eBay occasionally, you can find merchandise to sell at garage and estate sales, flea markets, and secondhand stores. But when it comes to selling a consistent number of items, you need to find a supplier that can provide you with a steady source of merchandise. That way you can sell year-round and not have all of your inventory dependent on weather or other seasonal factors.

51. Find a business address and get a tax ID number or reseller's certificate. This tells wholesalers that you have a legitimate business name such as a DBA (Doing Business As—a formal way of declaring that you are doing business under a different name than your own). It also enables the wholesalers to tell the IRS why they didn't charge you tax on what they sold you; rather, you are going to charge your customers sales tax. You should contact your state's Department of Revenue, which will provide you with the appropriate paperwork. You can then provide it to wholesalers who want to know you're "for real."

52. A business license and Tax ID do require some outlay. They might cost anywhere from $50 to $250, but they are essential items for you. You'll find links to each state's Department of Revenue and other appropriate business offices at www.worldwidebrands.com/wwb/tax_popup.asp.

53. You need a "real" street address and phone number for your business. Many wholesalers and other suppliers won't work with you unless you have one. A business address— even if your business is a booth in an antique mall—makes you look legitimate to wholesalers, who can be suspicious of online businesses.

54. Last but not least, you need a business bank account: a checking account that is separate from your personal account and that uses your business's name. You might have to keep a minimum balance on hand or be required to pay a service charge each month, but once you have a business bank account, you can use it to prove to wholesalers that you are a legitimate business concern.

FINDING A WHOLESALE SUPPLIER

55. It's important to find merchandise you are interested in and that you will enjoy selling on eBay. You might contact the manufacturer of the products you like yourself, and ask who the wholesalers are so you can contact them directly.

56. Before actually locating a wholesaler, your first job should be to identify a group of products you might want to sell and locate the manufacturers for them. Who manufactures the products you like? Get the real names and contact information from the owner's manual or the product packaging.

57. It's also important to locate wholesale suppliers who are willing and eager to work with small, home-based businesses. Most large wholesalers do not want to work with small home-based operators like you. Look for wholesalers who want to supply web-based sellers. You won't have to do so much work to convince them that you are a legitimate business entity.

58. When you do find the name and number of one of the wholesalers, call them up and ask to speak to a sales rep. Tell them the name of your business and where you're located. Tell them you would like to retail their products, and ask what they need to set up an account. They'll ask for your legal business name and your Tax ID number: have them ready.

59. Other information to include for a wholesale supplier: your projected sales volume per month, your credit reference numbers, and the amount of time you've been in business. Be honest about the fact that you're a home-based eBay seller. Come up with good, positive answers. Tell them you don't need credit but are willing to pay once a month with a credit card.

60. If you do approach a manufacturer, keep in mind that they really don't want to sell to retailers like you. They only want to sell to their middlemen—their wholesale suppliers. Don't ask them to sell directly to you (though it's tempting). Only ask them for contact information for one or two suppliers (they might be called distributors) who might be willing to work with you.

61. The suppliers you want to find are legitimate businesses with warehouses and employees rather than a single individual sitting at a home computer and functioning as a middleman. Whenever you contact a supplier, check their address and call the local Chamber of Commerce in their city to make sure they are reputable.

62. Also be sure to check out a supplier with the Better Business Bureau (www.bbb.org). Tell the BBB you are trying to "qualify" the supplier, which means you are trying to make sure they are qualified to work with you. (The supplier, of course, also wants to qualify you; it's a two-way street.)

63. Look for a wholesale supplier who can provide you with a steady supply of merchandise that you can sell all year round. This can supplement your sales of antiques, collectibles, and seasonal items and turn a sometime business into a full-time operation.

64. Look long and hard for drop-shippers. Ask around and get references; drop-shippers are worth the effort. A drop-shipper is a business that sells you wholesale merchandise but stores it for you in inventory and ships it out when you receive an order and relay it to them. (There's a whole section on drop-shippers later in this chapter.)

65. Once you've found one or two suppliers, it is tempting to quit hunting for others. Smart sellers are constantly searching for new sources of inventory, especially in high-volume areas like audio and video equipment and entertainment.

66. Most big wholesalers require you to buy a large amount of merchandise—probably much more than you want or have the ability to store. Try to get around this by finding a smaller, independent wholesaler who buys in quantity from manufacturers and who will let you share in a purchase. This way, you might only have to pay for half or one fourth of the entire purchase.

67. Rather than thinking of purchasing a single item, or a dozen items, get used to thinking in terms of the large quantities that wholesalers typically deal in. A liquidator might buy a pallet's worth of overstock items. The pallet consists of multiple cases, and you can buy one or more of those cases. Search the Web for wholesalers who will sell "case quantity," "by the pallet," or "by the lot."

68. You're just as likely to find a wholesaler by word of mouth as on the Internet. Ask people you know who are in business, either by email or in person. Troll the discussion forums and ask. Once you become a PowerSeller, you can access the PowerSeller discussion boards, where you can ask for suggestions on wholesalers.

APPROACHING WHOLESALERS

69. The personal touch matters when you're dealing with wholesalers, many of whom do business in an old-fashioned way. Check your local yellow pages for manufacturers in your area that you can visit in person.

70. If you do contact a wholesaler by email, make sure you use an email address that has your business's own domain name in it, not a free email service. Email addresses from yahoo.com and hotmail.com don't look "real" to wholesalers. Be polite in your email message and by all means proofread it before clicking the Send button.

71. You don't necessarily have to tell a wholesaler that you sell on the Internet. Some "old school" wholesalers look down on online sellers. They're worried that they're going to have to do a lot of hand-holding and helping sellers get set up with selling their products. Just give them your business name and location and leave it at that, unless you're specifically asked whether or not you sell online.

72. Don't be afraid to ask a wholesaler for samples you can inspect. You might even buy half a dozen items on a trial basis and put them up for sale on eBay to see how they do. Don't let a supplier bully you into buying ten gross (ten dozen dozens) or an entire pallet of merchandise before they'll do business with you. If a supplier won't send you samples to inspect, say no thanks and keep looking.

73. Pay attention to the source of the merchandise your wholesale supplier provides you with. Ask if these are items that customers have used and returned, and that might not work correctly or have some sort of manufacturing flaw, or if they are overstock items that haven't been used at all. Like many PowerSellers, you may want to only sell overstock, not returns.

74. Before you commit to making a purchase from a wholesaler, do some research on eBay and make sure the same sorts of items aren't being sold by lots of other sellers. It sounds obvious, but you need to make sure the field isn't already covered before you spend your money.

75. Most wholesale suppliers do not charge a fee to eBay sellers who want to use their services. They might charge you for a catalog or a CD that depicts their product line, just to cover their own costs in producing it. That kind of fee is understandable, and is not a service fee to provide you with merchandise to resell to the public on eBay.

76. If you don't have enough funds on hand to buy some initial stock, turn to American Express. You have to pay your bill in full in sixty days. That's enough time to make a purchase, receive the shipment, and put it up for sale on eBay. Hopefully you'll make back your initial investment in time to pay your charge bill.

77. If you buy a substantial quantity of merchandise from a wholesale supplier, that company should be able to send you stock photos of what you've purchased. That way you don't have to reinvent the wheel and take all your photos from scratch.

78. Sometimes it's difficult to get wholesale suppliers to take you seriously. Rent space in a booth in an antique mall and use that as your business address. It will look more official than your home address.

DROP-SHIPPING

79. Many eBay sellers dream of finding a drop-shipper. A drop-shipper is a supplier who stores your merchandise for you. You purchase merchandise, but you don't physically have it in your possession. When someone buys from you, you tell the drop-shipper, and they send out the item for you; you never actually touch the merchandise yourself.

80. At some point, you're going to need images of the products you sell. Drop-shippers realize that you need such photos, and most will provide you with zip archives or CDs that contain such images. In case you set up an account with a wholesaler that does not do this, you'll need to ask for samples and take the photos yourself. You can copy the images from another website, but be aware that this violates the site's copyright on its web content.

81. Expect to pay higher per-unit prices to a drop-shipper than you would to another traditional supplier who ships to you. After all, the shipper has to do the storage, the picking, the packing, and the labeling, and get the items to the shippers.

82. One problem with drop-shippers is lack of inventory. You don't want to send your drop-shipper a list of customers, only to be told that the items aren't in stock and there's going to be a delay. Get a report that states just how big an inventory the drop-shipper has on hand.

83. Backorders—requests from your customers that can't be fulfilled because the drop-shipper says they are out of stock—are inevitable. You have two choices: you can tell the customer that they'll have to wait, and be prepared for the unhappy response, or you can get a few samples of all of your drop-shipper's product line and keep them on hand in your home or office for just such occasions. You might have to purchase the samples yourself, but when the drop-shipper says the product isn't there, you can ship it out yourself.

84. Beware of individuals who advertise themselves as "agents" for drop-shippers and who want to charge you a fee for connecting you with a drop-shipper. You want to deal directly with the drop-shipper and not with a middleman. A real drop-shipper has a warehouse and a physical building, as well as a loading dock.

GARAGE SALES

85. The key to success with garage sales is to get to the right places first. Scour your local papers and look for sales that begin on a Thursday or Friday morning. If you can get there one of those mornings, you'll have less competition and increase your chances of actually finding something.

86. Always bargain at garage sales. Ask for a bulk discount if you're buying a large amount of merchandise. The worst you can hear is no.

87. Estate sales are usually the best type of house sale. Such events are typically advertised in the local paper days in advance. Some professionals manage to squeeze into such sales the night before. If you have nerve, you might be able to talk your way in.

88. Take a team approach to garage sales. Go to big sales with a partner who can help with shopping and carrying. Also consider splitting up; two or three people can cover a large metropolitan area faster than one.

89. If you can't get into a garage or estate sale before the official opening, expect to wait in line very early in the morning to gain entry when the sale opens. Consider hiring a student to stand in line for you. Moments before the sale starts, you can arrive, well-rested and ready for some intense—but potentially profitable—shopping.

90. Focus your garage sale efforts on older, affluent neighborhoods. Stay away from sales that emphasize baby clothes and toys; they're likely to be held by young couples who don't have valuable collectibles to sell.

91. When you're heading home at the end of the day, consider one more trip to a big sale. If you arrive during the hour before the sale ends, the sellers are likely to be tired and not looking to pack up what's left. They'll be only too happy to unload it for a song. The most desirable items will already be gone, but you can probably still find some things you can resell on eBay.

OTHER SOURCING RESOURCES

92. Brand names are all-important on eBay. If you do your sourcing at flea markets or secondhand stores, always gravitate toward items with recognizable names like Harley Davidson, Disney, or the like. Write a list of in-demand brands and take the list with you when you go out hunting.

93. Look up trade shows in your area of business. These are mass gatherings where wholesale suppliers meet retailers. In other words, they're tailor-made for eBay sellers like you to meet suppliers.

94. If you do attend a trade show, take your cell phone. Keep in touch with someone who is at a computer that's connected to the Internet. Call them up to research brand names and product names on eBay. Your goal is to determine if anyone else is selling the items, and to see if there's any demand for either that specific product or for that type of item.

95. Here's another way to gain credibility: list your eBay business in the phone book. This is an especially good way to attract attention from clients who want to hire you to sell for them on eBay.

96. Look for special promotions such as two-for-one deals at your local warehouse store. Sam's Club and Costco deal in bulk, and you can often pick up two, three, or four of something at a deep discount. You can sell one of those items on eBay and make back what you originally paid—possibly even more.

97. Dollar stores are great for many reasons. You can probably find a number of items there that you can resell for a profit on eBay. Everyone who does shipping needs packing tape, for instance. Buy ten rolls for $10, and resell them on eBay for $20. You'll still be selling them for less than what you would pay in a retail store.

98. Look around your local area for going-out-of-business sales and liquidations. Businesses usually have a special permit displayed in the window that allows them to have such a sale. You're sure to get great deals there. Don't be reluctant to ask for discounts on bulk purchases, either. The more you purchase, the more you can sell on eBay.

99. Liquidators are businesses that receive merchandise that has been returned or taken off the shelf for some reason. If you have a sales tax ID number and a warehouse full of storage space, you can be a liquidator yourself; you'll need to contact trucking companies and retailers to receive such merchandise, but you can get it at cut-rate prices and sell for big profits. Do a search on the Web for keywords such as "liquidation" and "salvage."

100. You say you don't have a Goodwill store in your area? Never fear: point your web browser to www.shopgoodwill.com and look for bargains there.

101. Can't sell that item because it's old or broken? Consider bundling it with something similar or complementary. A two-for-one sale or sale of a grouped lot might work better.

102. Look at trade publications to get an inside view of the industry you want to sell in. You are also likely to find ads from wholesalers who are looking for retailers to sell their wares.

103. Storage units have to be rented by the month. If the renters fall behind on their payments, the contents of those storage units are auctioned off. Attend those auctions: you are likely to find many profitable items you can sell on eBay.

104. Cities, states, and other governmental agencies frequently hold their own auctions. Call those agencies or surf their websites to find out when those sales are. Even if you only find a handful of items to resell at auction, it can be worth the time and effort.

3.

Selling on Consignment

When you're starting out as an eBay seller, you face many different challenges. Among these are the need to find desirable merchandise to sell and the need to build up positive feedback quickly by completing many transactions. One way to jump-start your eBay sales career is to post items for sale on behalf of their owners. When you sell for other people, you find you have less of a problem locating merchandise to sell on eBay. On the other hand, your life becomes more complicated in other ways. A new set of challenges arises that those who sell only for themselves never think about. You can do this kind of selling on an informal basis, or you can apply to eBay to become a member of their Trading Assistants Program.

105. Advertise yourself as a trading assistant, either on eBay itself or in your local area, so customers can come to you with merchandise to sell.

106. Much of your consignment business is likely to come from your local neighborhood. Simply spreading the word at block parties or other gatherings will bring you some business. Also, drop your business card off at your local neighborhood association. This group might need some fund-raising revenue itself, and you can offer to sell for them on eBay.

107. Set limits and stick to your fees. Spell out your arrangements clearly up front. Try to make a minimum of $10 on each sale. (I'm not talking about a sale price of $10, but about your fee as a consignment seller.)

108. Don't waste your time or that of your potential clients. Only sell items that will attract a substantial price on eBay, such as $25 or $50. "Screen" the items they hand over, and weed out the ones you don't think will be desirable.

109. eBay isn't always the best or easiest place to sell big items like furniture or exercise equipment. Shipping can be a nightmare. If someone comes to you with such an item to sell, point them to the local version of the free classified ad service Craigslist (www.craigslist.org) instead.

110. If you sell for other people on consignment, either as a trading assistant or as the owner or manager of a drop-off store, you can expect to run into customers who just aren't happy with the way their transactions go. I once had a drop-off store owner tell me that it wouldn't be a normal day if she didn't get yelled at, at least once. Develop a thick skin, and don't take complaints personally. Do your best to satisfy your customers, and when you've done your best, move on to the next sale.

111. Once you start selling on eBay, you're likely to be approached by family and friends asking you to sell something for them. Use your common sense: don't overburden yourself with such requests. Don't be reluctant to tell others that you charge a percentage (25 to 30 percent of the sales price is not uncommon). Also consider charging a small handling fee to cover shipping materials and your own time and effort.

112. If a friend or relative asks you to sell something, make sure you actually have the object in your possession. You don't want someone to tell you they've changed their mind about having the item sold on eBay after the purchase has been made. Also, make an inspection of the object. Once, I sold an automobile mirror on behalf of a relative who said it was in "mint condition." The buyer complained that it had two small flaws, and demanded a full refund. I gave the refund after receiving the item back in the mail, and I discovered that the mirror did indeed have two small dents in it that I hadn't noticed originally. In such a case you, the seller, risk negative feedback, not the object's owner.

113. If you sell for others, be sure to include a legal disclaimer in your descriptions that states you are not the owner or seller, but are acting on their behalf. This protects against selling stolen merchandise.

BECOMING A TRADING ASSISTANT

114. After you sell for others on an informal basis, consider joining eBay's official Trading Assistant Program. Find out more at tradin gassistant.ebay.com/ws/eBayISAPI.dll?Trading Assistant&page=main. You get a listing in eBay's Trading Assistant Directory and a chance to market your service to a wider audience than you could ever attract on your own.

115. Make sure you meet the requirements for becoming a Trading Assistant: you need to have sold at least ten items in the past three months, a feedback score of 100 or higher, a 97 percent positive feedback rating, and an eBay account in good standing.

116. You know that friends, family, and neighbors can be clients when you sell on consignment. But don't forget about local governments that need to unload surplus merchandise. Many municipalities have cars, trucks, and other merchandise they could sell for much-needed extra income. Contact your local city or county government and offer your services—if you're lucky, you might get a lot of merchandise to sell on an ongoing basis.

117. Nonprofit organizations such as schools and social agencies regularly hold fund-raisers. Approach them with an eye toward holding their fund-raisers on eBay. You'll spread goodwill, do a good deed, and build up lots of positive feedback that can help you in the future.

118. Local businesses almost always have overstock that they would love to sell. Many of them know that such merchandise is commonly sold on sites like eBay and Overstock.com. They're just waiting for someone to approach them and handle the actual sales activities for them. Approach your business associates and local businesses in your area to offer your services.

119. You don't have to commit to sell anything and everything, whether you're a Trading Assistant or an informal consignment seller. As an official Trading Assistant, you can specialize in three of eBay's main categories, and five subcategories for each of those three. Specializing in one area is a good way to stand out from the competition and make a name for yourself.

MARKETING YOURSELF AS A TRADING ASSISTANT

120. Register your trading assistant business with your neighborhood Chamber of Commerce. Ask them for advice on local businesses that periodically have liquidation needs and that might want to sell on eBay.

121. Take some time to craft a positive and welcoming profile in the Trading Assistants directory. You'll be competing with other Trading Assistants in your area, so you need to stand out from the crowd and make a good impression.

122. There's no charge for listing yourself in the Trading Assistants Directory. There is also no set formula for how much you should charge your clients. Take a look at other profiles in the directory and decide whether you should create a policy for how many times you should try to resell something, a policy on how to handle returns and refunds, and fees for various services.

123. Before you advertise your services as a Trading Assistant, make sure you are aware of any regulations regarding businesses that sell professionally on eBay. My own state, Illinois, has instituted regulations governing drop-off stores. Their owners have to take a course and pay a fee to obtain an auctioneer's license. It's not clear whether Illinois or other states with similar license regulations will try to impose the same requirements on Trading Assistants, but they might.

124. Add a phrase or sentence to all of your eBay descriptions to mention the fact that you are an official eBay Trading Assistant. Also mention this fact on your About Me page. It will build trust among bidders of your auctions, even if it doesn't steer you more consignment sales business.

125. When you do become a Trading Assistant, you should take advantage of the Trading Assistant toolkit: a set of posters and signs that you can copy to your computer, customize with your own contact information, and post on bulletin boards and in public places where you can attract potential clients.

126. When you're trying to sell your services to family, friends, or people in your local area, consider printing out your completed sales and saving them in a booklet that you can show. This is especially helpful for those who aren't at ease with computers.

127. It's to your advantage to make yourself available as a Trading Assistant to everyone, from individual consumers to businesses. However, if you only want to attract business clients, you can do so. Just uncheck the "Consumers" option in your profile page in the Trading Assistants directory, and your listing will only be visible to those eBay members who describe themselves as businesses.

128. Consider printing up a postcard with your eBay Trading Assistants logo and your business's name and contact information. Send the card to local businesses that might need your services. Follow up with a phone call to decision makers in the company.

129. Send the card not when business is slow, but when things are moving fast—just before businesses tend to purchase new inventory. For a business that deals in summer-related merchandise, this would be winter; for a business that makes most of its income over the holidays, this would be late summer or early fall.

OPERATING EFFICIENTLY AS A TRADING ASSISTANT

130. When you become a Trading Assistant, you gain access to a new level of support, and you become part of a new community. Be sure to participate in (or at least read) the Trading Assistants discussion forum. On the Trading Assistants home page, click Discussion Forums to get a link to all of the many workshops that have been held on eBay, especially for those who are listed as Trading Assistants.

131. When you sell on eBay for many clients as well as for yourself, you need to have a well-organized storage area. Be sure to keep items from different clients in clearly marked areas so they don't get mixed up.

132. When you sell for others, make sure your homeowner's or renter's insurance covers damage to the eBay sales merchandise due to fire, flood, or other disasters. If it doesn't, you should ask for a supplemental rider and pay a little extra. The peace of mind is worth it, especially when others' possessions are involved.

133. When you're busy selling for many people who are in a hurry (including yourself), you need to make use of all the technical shortcuts you can find. Create listing templates using a tool like Listing Designer; try to create different color or type schemes for each client so that person feels unique and special. Also make use of tools like Turbo Lister and Blackthorne Assistant, and the Inserts feature in the Sell Your Item form.

134. If you want to build a good reputation by conducting charity sales events, you have to conduct the sales on eBay in one of two ways: you run the sale through eBay Giving Works (www.givingworks.com), or you obtain a signed letter of consent from the organization and post it along with your sales descriptions.

135. If you're lucky, you might find consignment customers who want to do more than have you sell for them. They might want you to *buy* for them on eBay. Charge them the same sales commission as you do for selling. It's easy money for you, and it will probably save them some time and money in the long run as well.

136. You'll attract more bidders if you are able to offer buyer financing. You can do this automatically if you accept PayPal payments and your buyers are both U.S. citizens and PayPal members. If you use eBay's Sell Your Item form, choose the Buyer Financing option from the Payment and Shipping page. The Buyer Financing option automatically appears if you already accept PayPal or offer something for a starting bid of more than $199.

137. Whether you sell on consignment informally, as a Trading Assistant, or through a drop-off store, be patient. You will probably have to teach your customers the basics about how eBay works. You'll probably have to state the same kinds of talking points over and over again. Remember that part of your job is to be a teacher and a good representative for eBay as well as your own business.

STARTING A DROP-OFF STORE

138. Location, location, location: it's one of the most important decisions you have to make. Pick a well-traveled location, such as a busy intersection. Also pick an area where parking is readily available: you don't want foot traffic, you want cars to be able to park where you are.

139. You want your drop-off store to be a destination location—a place where people will drive to from a distance. Locate it in an area that is already a destination, such as a strip mall or popular shopping area.

140. Make sure your store has plenty of storage space. You'll need a room to meet customers, a room for photography and wrapping, and at least one room for storage.

141. Make sure you have a loading/drop-off area. It's essential for those customers who have motorcycles or other heavy items to sell.

142. Drop-off stores are great for people who have high-ticket items like boats to sell. They'll make you a big commission. Make sure you have a parking space or two at your disposal, if not a parking lot.

143. A drop-off store requires someone with computer expertise to network and maintain two or more computers. One is needed for each employee.

144. Be sure to store your customers' personal information in a secure location. The information should be on a drive that is separate from the Internet, so hackers can't break into it.

145. PayPal isn't good enough when you run a store. To accept credit cards, you'll need an account with a financial institution or online merchant service. You'll also need a card reader, a terminal that connects you to the credit card network.

146. One drop-off store I know has two computer screens connected to a single computer. One screen is for the employee, the other for the customer. The moment the customer brings in an item to sell, the employee researches it on eBay. That way, both can see if it will sell for the $50 minimum.

147. A website is a must for any drop-off store. Yours should explain who you are, how the sales process works, where you are located, and examples of your recent eBay success stories.

148. You don't have to sell everything that comes into your store. Most stores won't handle anything that isn't likely to fetch a minimum of $50.

149. For big and bulky items such as couches or appliances, it can be more trouble to sell on eBay than the item is actually worth. You can list the item on Craigslist (www.craigslist.com) and specify that the customer has to pick the item up, or list it on eBay and specify local pickup. If those items are too much trouble for you, urge the customer to place a listing on Craigslist.

150. When you open a drop-off store, new advertising and marketing opportunities appear. For instance, you can take out an ad in your local Yellow Pages, or post a notice in the local grocery store.

151. To get a jump start with a new drop-off business, consider opening a franchise. That way you can build on someone else's success and recognizable name.

4.

Capturing Clear Digital Images

If you've ever seen an eBay auction without any kind of photo accompanying it, you know why photos are so important. An auction that lacks images just isn't attractive. While descriptions and details prompt bids, images are what attract the attention of buyers. They also help buyers decide just how interested they are in the merchandise being offered. Not only that, but they help buyers verify the claims you are making in your descriptions. This chapter presents tips that will help you take clear images to accompany your sales listings on eBay.

152. Set up a photo studio where you can quickly set up and capture digital images. Keep your studio separate from the rest of your house, and lock the space so your kids can't get at it. Having a designated photo area will make the photography aspect of creating descriptions go much quicker.

153. When buying a digital camera, don't "focus" solely on megapixels. Look closely at the camera's capacity to take clear close-ups. Ask about the macro capability. How close can the camera focus? How well does the zoom work?

154. Make sure you have enough server space to store all of your photos. You don't want to eat up your profits by being over-charged when you run out of your allotted space. Consider using a free photo hosting service.

155. Whether you use tungsten, halogen, or regular incandescent light, look in your camera's instruction manual to find the "white balance" control. Set the white balance to match the type of light you use, and you'll get better results.

FOUR FREE OR LOW-COST PHOTO HOSTING SERVICES

156. If you use America Online to get online, you are probably aware that you can have up to seven separate "screen names." You may not be aware that each one of those screen names comes with 2MB of space. That's 14MB overall. You can create screen names like Hosting1, Hosting2, and so on, and use each for hosting your eBay auction photos.

157. The Auction-Images.com site (http://www.auction-images.com) gives you 1MB of storage space for free. That's not a lot, but it can help you get started on eBay. There's also a 2MB hosting package for $1 per month and 10MB for $5 per month. eBay Motors images are not allowed, however.

158. Boomspeed.com (http://www.boom speed.com), like many other hosting sites, no longer has a free storage option. However, you can still get one of the best deals around: for $6 a month, you get 100MB of storage space.

159. Vendio Image Hosting (http://www.vendio.com) charges a little more than other photo hosts: $2.95 per month for 3MB and $9.95 per month for 55MB. The better deal comes if you open a Vendio Store (Vendio's equivalent of an eBay Store), which costs roughly $21 per month depending on the number of items you sell. Then you get 135MB of photo storage for no additional charge.

PRESENTATION IS EVERYTHING!

160. Good photo presentation can help make a lackluster item look better. The most important part of your presentation is the background. If you take your photos indoors, get one or two sheets or pieces of cardboard that are in a solid color. One should be dark in color, the other light. Use the dark color for light or clear objects; use the light background for everything else.

161. Sometimes, the key to a good presentation is simply avoiding the obvious photo "don'ts." Don't place something in front of an ugly wall with peeling paint or distracting wallpaper, don't take the photo outdoors with lots of distracting landscape in the background, don't point a flash directly at a shiny object.

162. Invest in several table stands if you sell jewelry or other small items. Accessories look better if they are mounted and presented in an eye-catching way on clear plastic stands rather than sitting flat on a table. The stands also make it easier for you to photograph the items.

163. Be sure you take the time to clean your item before you photograph it. If it's silver or gold, polish it. If it's dirty, give it a good wash. You don't want your shoppers complaining about dirt embedded in your item, and you don't want to discourage people from bidding just because you haven't put your item in the best light.

164. If you don't have a home photo studio and lots of lights, you can take photos outside. Daylight that isn't too bright and sunny can be excellent for photos. Try to take your outdoor photos on days when it's overcast but still bright. Or, if it's bright and sunny out, arrange your merchandise under an umbrella (such as the umbrella that commonly shades a patio table) to diffuse the light and prevent distracting reflections.

165. I've gone back and forth with several of my photographer friends about the best light for eBay photos. I used to think halogen light was the brightest and clearest, but, after having used it myself, I have to say that while it's bright, it is cold and creates glare. A mixture of halogen and incandescent lights pointed from different angles might be best. The important thing is to provide light from two or more different directions to reduce shadows.

166. If you sell the same type of merchandise over and over, come up with a routine for showing the item for several different angles. It will help you take photos quickly, which is important if you have ten or twelve items you want to get online and you want to start the sale in just a few hours. For your first photo, take a straight-on shot that will serve as your Gallery photo; then take a close-up of the front, a profile, an underneath shot, and so on.

167. In the chapter on revising photos, I mention that cropping images (deleting unnecessary background areas) is one of the best ways to edit and improve them. That's true. But to save time, use the zoom control to make your objects fill up the viewfinder in your camera. Just leave a little bit of background around the object. That way, you won't have to crop it at all.

168. If you sell clothing, make sure it's clean when you put the sale online. Invest in a steamer or high-quality iron if you sell dresses, shirts, or other clothing items. Get a shoe polish kit if you sell shoes. Remember, all of these supplies are deductible at tax time.

169. If you sell jewelry, rings, or other small items, consider buying some modeling clay (the kind that doesn't harden when exposed to air). You can push the items into the clay and they won't slip around, so they'll be easier to arrange and photograph.

170. If you take photos of glass, mirrors, silver, or other highly reflective items, make sure something doesn't show up in the reflection that you don't want people to see. This includes you or other members of your family. It sounds strange, but there's an odd subculture of people who are obsessed with looking for reflections in eBay items, and some even take "naughty" photos of themselves in reflections and try to get them online.

171. When it comes to cleaning, one of the best things you can buy is a liquid called Goo Gone. It removes prices written in marker, the sticky residue of adhesive tape and stickers, and other leftovers that make an item look worse than it is.

172. An ordinary pencil eraser can be a surprisingly good cleaner. For smudges and scratches on suede, it's excellent.

173. Simply changing the background can make a dramatic improvement in the quality of your photos. For shiny objects like jewelry and silverware, a dark background makes the object "jump out" at the viewer. For many dark or neutral-colored objects, a white or beige background is far better than a cluttered living room or other location where household furnishings are visible.

FINDING THE RIGHT DIGITAL CAMERA

174. If you're looking for a camera to use for family photos and portraits, get one that can handle as many megapixels as possible. If you want the camera only for use on eBay, it's perfectly fine to get a secondhand one that can only capture 2 or 3 megapixels. You only need to capture 640 x 480 (307,200 pixels, or less than a third of one megapixel) because most monitors can't display any more than that.

175. Your digital camera might be able to capture 4, 5, 6 or even more megapixels' worth of detail. But you don't need all that power for an image that's only designed to appear on eBay. Set your resolution to 680 x 480, which is good enough for the Web and keeps your images as small and manageable as possible.

176. The ability to zoom in and out on an image is one of the most important qualities you should look for in a digital camera. Find a camera with an easy-to-use zoom feature—test to see how close you can get to the object without having to switch to your macro focus feature. If you can get about six inches away and the image is still sharp, you'll save time when taking close-ups.

177. Super close-ups that are sharp and clear really sell products. Your camera's macro function enables you to get as close as possible. The best digital cameras can get one or two inches from an object and focus clearly. By all means buy a digital camera with a good macro feature.

178. When you're shopping for digital cameras, it's not a bad idea to go to a real brick-and-mortar store to touch and feel and try out the different models. But when it comes to actually buying, think about eBay. You might find the best prices on your very own favorite auction site. And when you make a purchase, you get positive feedback that you can add to your overall feedback rating.

179. Sometimes, digital cameras aren't the best solution. If you're trying to take a photo of a flat paper object, such as a map or a photo, you may be better off scanning the object on a flatbed scanner. If you don't have a scanner yourself, you can use one at FedEx Kinko's or another service bureau for a nominal fee.

CAMERA ACCESSORIES

180. The built-in memory cards that come with some digital cameras don't hold many digital images. After only twenty or thirty images, you have to install a new card. Spend some money (less than $100) and buy a new memory card so you can take sixty, seventy, or more photos before you have to transfer them to your computer. Again, the up-front expense will save you time in the long run.

181. Tired of bending over, sitting down, and moving around when you're trying to take dozens of photos at a time? It can take a toll on your back. Invest in a tripod with three extendable legs so you can fix the camera in one position and save the wear and tear on your body. Make sure you find a tripod that has a quick release feature and a hinge that lets you change the angle of the camera, too.

182. Batteries are another one of those things that cost money up front but save you money in the long run. Buy one of those rechargeable battery packs if your camera didn't already come with one. You don't want to waste time and money replacing those AA- or AAA-size batteries every few weeks.

CREATING A PHOTO STUDIO

183. Invest in several different backgrounds that will contrast with your merchandise and make it easier to see. Also, buy a couple of stands for jewelry or other small items.

184. This sounds really simple-minded, but it's something I learned from hard experience: give yourself a way to sit down when you take photos. When you're taking a hundred or more photos, it's much less tiring. Sitting down while taking your photos makes it easier to keep them in focus, too.

185. Many eBay sellers create a "photo tent" that they place around the items they want to sell. You can make a homemade tent by hanging a white cloth on some poles or furnishings; you can also buy a small specially designed tent on eBay. A tent not only creates an even white background, it also diffuses the light and reduces glare.

186. For tiny items like coins, rings, and watches, a milk jug will also work. The jug has to be cut open a bit at the top, and you place your camera lens inside the hole. The item goes at the bottom of the jug. You'll see a photo posted on eBay as part of a photography workshop at forums.ebay.com/db2/thread.jspa? threadID=1000030045.

187. Set aside a room in your house, or a corner of a room, that is designated solely for the purpose of taking photos of your eBay auction merchandise. You won't have to clean up the area every time you want to start a bunch of sales. Just turn on the lights, get your camera ready, and you're good to go.

188. Don't depend on your digital camera's built-in flash to provide you with all the lighting you need for your eBay photography. Invest in some extra lamps and point them at your photography table from different angles. IKEA, the Swedish furniture megastore, has halogen lamps that cost less than $20 and will provide strong, clear light.

189. If you sell clothing, it's often much more attractive to present it on a human figure rather than a table. Some sellers model their own clothes in their photos. If you're camera-shy, invest in a mannequin. Often, eBay itself is the best place to find such an item.

PROCESSING YOUR DIGITAL PHOTOS

190. Your impulse is probably to take your digital photos in one of your camera's built-in JPEG formats. When I take photos, however, I take them in TIFF (Tagged Image File Format), which gives better quality. I use my graphics program (Paint Shop Pro) to convert them to JPEG format so they can be viewed on the Web. It's an extra step, but I believe my photos come out better because of it.

191. I make sure to keep my images as small as possible. TIFF images can be huge in size if you take them at high resolution. I take them at 640 x 480 to begin with. When I convert them to JPEG, they end up at an average of 20K or 30K each in size.

192. Come up with a numbering system for your photos that's easy to remember and implement. I do my numbering in terms of batches. Within each batch, I have an item number, and then the number of the photo itself. My numbers look like this (this example is for item number two in batch ten): 10-2-1.jpg, 10-2-2.jpg, and so on.

193. Save a copy of your photos on your computer as well as on the server to which you subscribe to host your images. It's useful to have photos that you can view and access quickly, especially if you want to relist something you listed a few weeks before and you can't remember the batch or item number. You can scroll through your local photo archives and find it quickly.

194. All those photos on your server can take up a lot of space. If your photo host (or your web hosting service) only allocates, say, 500MB of disk space, you should check every few weeks to make sure you're not going over your limit. If you do, you'll probably be charged extra. Delete photos from the server after items are sold; always keep a copy on your computer for a backup.

195. When you're numbering photos, take a look at them. Make note of any images that are too blurry, too bright, or that have other flaws. You should retake them at some point so they show your items in their best light (literally).

196. Numbering photos, both on your computer and in your sales software (Turbo Lister, for instance), is a time-consuming process. I save a set of sales in my software as a template. Each template has a set of six or seven images associated with it. When it comes time to edit the template listings and add new photos, I don't have to retype all the photo URLs from scratch; I just change the batch numbers and item numbers. If you're adding a hundred photos per night, this saves a lot of time and trouble.

197. Even though your high-tech digital camera can capture 5, 6, or more megapixels' worth of digital information, the average computer screen can't display it. Save the high resolution for photos you want to print and hang on a wall. For eBay auction photos, use the coarsest resolution you have, which is probably 640 x 480. It will keep your file size low, and it's all the average monitor can display, anyway.

198. Once you've gone through the time and effort required to take good photos, protect them so they aren't copied and reused by other sellers. Yes, it happens: photos used in one person's auction show up in the auction of another seller who is selling the same item. You can add an icon to your photo using a graphics program. Type the text in a program such as Paint Shop Pro, make the text transparent, and copy it and paste it over your photos.

5.

Creating Descriptions That Attract Buyers

Photos are important tools when it comes time to sell merchandise on eBay, but good descriptions are equally important. Often, the thing that sets a PowerSeller apart from other sellers is the time and effort that member spends on a good description. A good description is full of details, tells a story, and leaves the shopper feeling more interested after reading it. The more positive you are in your listing text, the more success you'll have on eBay. You don't have to be a professional writer to create good descriptions, either. Just follow the tips presented in this chapter.

199. Learn from other sellers. Take time to look through the descriptions of sellers you admire—even those you compete with directly. Don't be reluctant to imitate their colors, headings, photos, or layouts, as long as you're not directly copying them.

200. The Sell Your Item form is accessed by simply clicking Sell in the navigation bar at the top of any eBay page. The form is slow and tedious to use when you have eight, ten, twelve, or more items to get online at the same time. However, Sell Your Item does have some features that you won't find elsewhere. One is the ability to search sales categories by keyword. Another is the Inserts feature, which lets you save standard phrases, logos, and other items so you can enter them from a drop-down list.

201. You can always use the Sell Your Item form's category selection tool even if you don't use the Sell Your Item form to create your description. Click Sell in the eBay navigation bar. Click Sell Your Item, and log in. When the Sell Your Item: Select Category page appears, enter a keyword that describes your item, and click Search. Make note of the category or categories (you can choose two) that are returned. Enter them in Turbo Lister or whatever software you use to create auction listings.

202. Take some time up front to design a sales template for your listings. Consider hiring a designer to help you choose colors and typefaces that will complement your eBay business.

203. Anything you can say in your description about your level of experience as a seller, collector, or professional in your field will make shoppers feel better about placing a bid or making a purchase. Point out how long you've been selling, how many items you've sold, how long you've been a collector, or any honors or degrees you've received that pertain to your sales.

SEVEN ESSENTIAL TIPS FOR GREAT DESCRIPTIONS

204. Make sure your titles and descriptions contain keywords that will make your items show up in search results. Titles and keywords are so important that they're discussed in their own sections later in this chapter.

205. A few positive and well-chosen descriptive words go a long way toward ensuring that your merchandise sells. If you're selling a briefcase, say something like "sensible" or "compact." Such words make the object more attractive to prospective buyers.

206. Why include a description that's only a sentence or two long, or one that doesn't even use complete sentences in the first place? The more details you provide, the more "hooks" you give your prospective buyers, and the better your chances of making a sale. Do a little research about what you have to sell—even if it's only doing a search on eBay itself. Imagine that you don't have any photos at all and are forced to describe your item by words alone.

207. Be positive! Too many sellers seem to be apologetic about their descriptions. Tell people how much you love what you have to sell, or how you wish you could keep it, or what you used to do with it—or what *they* might do with it. Be a cheerleader for your merchandise, and you'll inspire shoppers to place bids.

208. Learn to speak the language your buyers are used to. The specialized collectors and dedicated shoppers who make eager bidders often speak with special terminology. I had never thought about things like a "toe box," "mules," "slides," "kilties," "shawls," or "cap toes" until I really got involved with selling shoes. I find such terms fascinating now, and I enjoy throwing them around in my descriptions as though I'm a professional shoe salesman (which, in fact, I am).

209. If you sell collectibles like coins, learn the grading system and what terms like "mint," "proof," "near mint," "very good," and "fair" really mean. Come up with a grading system so you can accurately describe the condition of what you have for sale.

210. Make sure you come up with a set of terms of sale that you include with each of your descriptions. Type it in a word processing document or as a template in Turbo Lister or another program so you don't have to re-enter it every time you put something up for sale. Terms of sale spell out the type of payment you will receive, when you expect to receive payment, and what your return policy is.

PHOTOS IN YOUR DESCRIPTIONS

211. Sometimes you don't need a gallery photo with your description. Usually, such thumbnail images are important; they help your description stand out on a page full of search results, for instance. But if your item has a recognizable brand name and is well-known to shoppers, they can look it up on the manufacturer's website.

212. Gallery photos cost 35 cents on auctions. However, if you list something in your eBay Store, each gallery photo only costs one cent.

213. A thumbnail image is free! A thumbnail is a small version of a larger photo—a gallery image is a perfect example. If you format your auction descriptions using HyperText Markup Language (HTML), the set of markup instructions used to create web pages, you can format a single image twice. Suppose your image file is named object.jpg, and you store your images at www.mysite.com/ebay. You could use the following HTML to format your image twice: <a href="http://www.mysite.com/ebay/object.jpg> <img src="http://www.mysite.com/ebay/object.jpg" WIDTH="275" Border="0"> </a>

This formats the image as a small thumbnail version that is 275 pixels wide. When a viewer clicks the image, his browser will display the full-size version. Just replace the URL for your own hosting service and the item's file name, and you can use this bit of HTML yourself in your auction descriptions.

SCHEDULING YOUR LISTINGS

214. Weekends are generally regarded as the best time to end your auction. Personally, I have the best luck with sales that end on Sunday evenings. But Wednesdays are a good evening, too. And on certain weeks, I've had a better sell-through rate on Tuesday or Thursday than I do on Sunday. Experiment by listing small batches of items several nights a week for several weeks to see what the best days are for you.

215. Is there a more systematic way to determine the best day of the week to end an eBay auction (besides Sunday, that is)? I searched for people selling shoes to find the answer. Click Advanced Search, check Completed Items, and enter the User ID of one of your rival sellers. See when their sales end, and when most of their sales occur. That's how I settled on Wednesday as a good alternative to Sunday for my type of merchandise (shoes).

216. If you want your sales to end on a particular day, such as Sunday, you have two or three chances to do so. Normally, I list a group of items on Sunday night in seven-day auctions that end the following Sunday. But two days later, on Tuesday night, I often list some more items for sale. This time, I hold five-day auctions. They'll end the same night: Sunday. If you have some really "hot" items, you can list them at a three-day auction, too.

217. Sometimes it pays to schedule the ending time of an auction to match the items you're selling. If you are selling office equipment or supplies, don't end the sale on a weekend, for instance. Make the process easy on the corporate purchasing officers you're trying to reach, and end the sale on a weekday during working hours (9 a.m.–5 p.m.).

218. What's the best time of day to end a sale, whether you end it on a Sunday or not? Usually, I end my sales at 9–10 p.m. in my Central Time Zone in the United States. But I've sold plenty of items to bidders in Europe, where the sale is ending in the wee hours of the morning. To take those bidders into account, it might be better to end the sale on a Saturday or Sunday afternoon. But ending it late at night doesn't hinder overseas buyers from participating. Automated bidding software means they don't need to be present at their computers at the end of a sale. Bottom line: end the sale when it's convenient for you. The time is *always* convenient to a buyer who really wants what you have to offer.

219. eBay periodically offers special promotions that can save you some money. Often, these promotions fall on holidays. You might be able to take advantage of a "One-Cent Gallery Photos Day" or a "Ten-Cent Fixed Price Sale" deal. You'll find out about such events if you visit the Announcements board (http://www2.ebay.com/aw/marketing.shtml).

CREATING GOOD TITLES

220. A good title makes full use of the fifty-five-character limit. Be specific and come up with as many descriptive words as you can. By all means, include the manufacturer name and brand name. Model numbers work, as well as colors and sizes. A word or two about the condition is useful if the condition is "mint," "like new," or "NIB" (New in Box). Avoid fillers like "For Sale" (everybody knows you're putting the item up for sale), or "L@@K."

221. A great title will include something that sets your item apart from the others up for sale on eBay. (You'll quickly discover that it's rare to be the only one selling the item you have; it's more common to find that you have lots of competition.) If your item is rare, made of sterling silver, or made in Italy, say that in the title if you can fit it in.

222. You can encourage your prospective buyers to feel the same way you do about an item. I've found that putting a nice pair of shoes up for sale isn't always enough. Words like "classy," "sporty," "elegant," or "wild and crazy" help get people's emotions engaged and get them to feel something about what you're selling.

223. Perhaps the best way to learn what works and what doesn't in terms of titles is to do a Completed Items search for items that are similar to what you have to sell. You don't have to copy someone else's title exactly to get some good ideas for keywords and descriptive turns of phrase.

224. When you're writing a title, try to avoid abbreviations if at all possible. A title that includes a phrase like "Esp. Maker" for "Espresso Maker" means that the important keyword "espresso" won't show up in keyword searches. Your auction won't be found as often, and this reduces the number of bids you'll receive.

225. It's expensive (50 cents) to add a subheading to an auction title, but it definitely makes your sale stand out from others around it. Use a subheading when you have something important to add that you couldn't fit in the title and that is likely to increase interest—that your item is a rare color, that it comes in its original box, and so on.

226. Get to know your abbreviations—they can help you cram a little more important information into your titles. Terms like NR (No Reserve), NIB (New in Box), and others are well-known to bidders and will quickly be recognized by them.

227. Be sure to include spelling variations in your auction titles. For instance, along with "version 3," you might include "v. 3" and "ver. 3." Along with "F-150," include "F150" as well. Your sale will show up in a wider range of search results than it would otherwise.

228. Capital letters in titles are frequently overused. If you have one or two key words you need to emphasize in your title, put them in ALL CAPS and you'll get attention. But don't do the entire title in caps.

229. Some of the most desirable words you can insert in an auction title, aside from a recognizable and desirable brand name, are "New" and "Like New." Everyone knows what "New" means. But be careful not to overuse "Like New." "Like New" really means that something is basically new but has perhaps been used (or worn) once or twice and no longer has its price tag. There is no serious wear at all on the item. If the item is "Like New," use terms like "Mint" or "XLNT" (for excellent).

ADDING KEYWORDS TO YOUR DESCRIPTIONS

230. One of the most important elements you can include in a title is a keyword—an item that shoppers are going to enter in eBay's search box when they're searching for what you have to sell. Include as many keywords in the title as you can. "Old Rolex Watch" is short and sweet. But "1948 Gold Rolex Oyster Perpetual Wristwatch w/Band" is better not only because it's more specific but has more keywords, which increases the chances that shoppers will actually find it.

231. Purchase a few eBay Keywords to improve your eBay Store's visibility. Also consider buying some Google AdWords to provide extra exposure for your store merchandise.

232. You definitely want to add keywords to your descriptions, but avoid keyword spamming, which can cause your description to be taken down by eBay. Typical keyword spamming is used by sellers who throw around highly desirable brand names that don't apply to the object being sold, such as "Guccy Wristwatch for Sale Not Gucci" or "Cort Bass Guitar Like Fender or Gibson."

233. If you're looking for the best keywords that pertain to items typically sold in your category of interest, turn to Seller Central. Click Category Tips (http://pages.ebay.com/sellercentral/sellbycategory.html). Consult the newsletter that pertains to the category in which you want to sell.

MAKE YOUR TONE MATCH YOUR MERCHANDISE

234. Suppose you have a joke or gag gift to sell on eBay. If you're selling something funny, make your email communications funny, too. Give your description a jaunty tone.

235. Suppose you are trying to sell a designer T-shirt or handbag for a teenager or someone who wants to keep up with the latest trends. It won't hurt to throw around a few words like "phat" in your description.

236. Suppose you're selling something that will only appeal to an effete or highbrow audience. Use precise, elevated language. Don't use contractions. Present the item in a dry, serious, straightforward tone.

237. If your primary audience is a set of knowledgeable collectors, give them what they want. Provide information about the item. Model numbers, dates, materials, colors, and anything you can say about what you have to sell will be eagerly perused by your audience. Try to throw in as many facts as you can; you're sure to hold their interest.

238. You can also make a dull item more interesting by writing a funny description. I once sold a boring old shoehorn by telling a story about how it began life in a famous department store and ended up in a lowly shoe box. Tell a story, and you're sure to attract bids.

239. If you don't actually own what you're selling, make that clear in the description. This absolves you, to some extent, from having to have a detailed knowledge of an item's history or manufacturer, or a detailed explanation of how it works. You'll still have to answer questions, but you can tell bidders that you'll have to consult with the item's actual owner when you do so, which may add time to the response. (Make sure you have a way to contact the owner when such questions occur.)

240. If you know that your cloth items—such as stuffed animals, plush toys, or clothing—came from a clean, smoke-free environment, it's a nice touch to add this to your description. On the other hand, if you're not sure where the merchandise came from, don't make this claim. Your buyer may have a more sensitive nose than you, and might be able to detect smoke when you can't.

241. No matter what you sell, measure it, and include the measurements in your descriptions. It makes you look meticulous and trustworthy, and it reduces the chances that your buyer will be surprised by something that doesn't fit or doesn't meet expectations.

242. The more measurements you can get, the better. For instance, when I'm measuring shoes, I often try to measure the inside size as well as the outside. If you don't find a size on clothing or other items you sell, detailed measurements can still help buyers know what they're getting.

243. There are all kinds of accessories that add value to what you're selling and should be mentioned in your description. These include the original box, the price tag, the original receipt, the warranty card, or instruction manuals.

244. Yes, you're in a hurry. Yes, the kids are crying upstairs and you haven't had your dinner yet. Yes, you're tired because you are doing eBay sales after a full day at work. Don't let your irritation and fatigue creep into your descriptions. Write in complete sentences, and be upbeat and friendly—no matter how you really feel.

CHOOSING THE RIGHT AUCTION FORMAT

245. One of the first things you have to decide when you're creating a description is what format your sale will take. Standard auctions have a starting price but no reserve. Reserve auctions have a reserve that you set and that is kept secret until someone's bid meets or exceeds it. A fixed-price sale is a Buy It Now price. Don't immediately assume you should hold a standard auction. If you only want to sell something for a certain price, choose the fixed-price format. Set a reserve if you need to protect your investment and want to get back what you originally paid for the item.

246. There's one more type of auction you need to consider: a multiple-item auction, sometimes called a Dutch auction. Choose the multiple-item format if you have two or more identical items to sell and you don't want to create a separate description for each one. Bidders have the option of bidding on more than one item; the lowest qualifying bidder gets to win your item. For example, if you have ten items for sale and eleven bidders bid on one item each, the eleventh bidder will be knocked out of the competition.

247. The very first time you create an auction, do a test. Create a sale and choose the Test category that eBay has provided just for sellers who want to get their sales online and make sure they do everything right without having to be charged an insertion fee. It's under the category "Everything Else." After you create your test auction, upload it to eBay, and then check it out to make sure the photos appear correctly and the formatting is just the way you want.

248. You can choose to list your item in a second category as well as the first. eBay claims that items have a better chance of selling when you do this, but listing in a second category doubles your insertion fee. If you sell something for a $9.99 starting price, your insertion fee jumps from 35 to 70 cents. In my opinion, you should only choose a second category for an item that doesn't fit obviously into any category and that is likely to sell for a high price.

249. Why would you want to sell an item in the seldom-used one-day format? It's perfect if you have concert tickets to sell right away, or even a tee time at a golf course. Also consider selling in this format if it's close to a big holiday and you have the perfect Valentine's Day or Mother's Day gift, for instance.

PRICING YOUR SALES

250. Pricing isn't always critical. As a general rule, I determine the lowest amount I am willing to accept for an item, and I use that as my starting price. I try to make $10 profit on each sale. Any less, and it isn't worth my time to write the description, take the photos, and ship the item. If I get more, so much the better.

251. Often, you turn away bidders if you have a high starting price. If you start with a low price (say, $9.99 or even 99 cents), you're likely to attract bids because the bidders feel like they're getting a bargain. Reserve prices aren't seen much on eBay anymore because you have to pay an extra $1 fee for reserve prices of $1 to $49.99, $2 for reserves of $50 to $199, and 1 percent of the reserve price if it is $200 or over.

252. Suppose you're not certain about pricing. You've always got the option of inviting a "Best Offer" from a buyer. You've got nothing to lose by checking the Best Offer option in either the Sell Your Item form, Turbo Lister, or other sales software. You can either accept or reject the offers you receive. Some sellers use this option all the time in their eBay Stores, and they improve their sales performance with it.

253. When should you offer a Buy It Now price as well as an auction price? Buy It Now prices cost extra, so only offer them on items that are especially desirable. Set a price you'll be happy with and that seems reasonable based on other, similar items that have sold on eBay in the recent past.

DESIGNING YOUR LISTINGS

254. The most obvious way to design a listing is to use eBay's own Listing Designer. It is made available to you either in the Sell Your Item form or in Turbo Lister. But you have to pay an extra 10 cent surcharge every time you use it. For casual sellers, Listing Designer makes sense. For committed sellers who put dozens or even hundreds of items online each month, it's costly. Design your own listings using bold or italic type, or with the use of tables.

255. A table is a feature of HTML (Hyper-Text Markup Language) that enables web page contents to be organized into rows and columns. Table borders—the lines that separate individual cells—don't have to be visible. The simplest kind of table contains one column and one row, and has borders set to 0 (in other words, it's not visible). The HTML for this is:

```
<table   border=0   cellspacing=0   width=80%
bgcolor=#FFFFFF>
<tr><td>
CONTENTS GO HERE
</td> </tr>
<table>
```

256. If you don't know how to add HTML to a text file and create a web page from scratch yourself, don't worry. Plenty of web page editors allow you to create tables without having to know HTML at all. Some of the most popular are Macromedia Dreamweaver (macromedia.com) and Microsoft FrontPage (office.microsoft.com/en-us/FX010858021033.aspx). I personally like Netscape Composer, which comes free with the Netscape web browser, or Mozilla Composer, which comes with Mozilla (www.mozilla.org).

257. Try different description layout, color, and type combinations to see which set appeals to your audience and results in the most bids. Professionals in marketing and advertising have known for years that different colors produce different responses. You might find that blue results in more sales than green or red, for instance.

258. Should you consider hiring a professional designer to create a listing template and a logo for your eBay sales? Plenty of full-time sellers do it. If you plan to sell on eBay for years at a time, a few hundred dollars might be worth the investment. Check out the sample eBay templates created by Debbie Levitt of As Was Design (http://aswas.com).

259. If you have two or more separate sales that contain complementary information—for example, one listing for expensive bedsheets and another for pillow covers—mention each item in the other item's listing. You might just encourage someone to purchase two things instead of just one.

260. One of the best ways to encourage multiple purchases is to mention that you'll be happy to combine shipping for two or more items. In other words, you'll ship two or more items in a single package so a buyer will save on shipping overall. Instead of having to pay two or more separate shipping charges, the buyer only has to pay one. That sort of thing makes buyers really happy.

261. When you figure out how to format your own auction listings using HTML, it becomes tempting to add "bells and whistles" such as background sounds or animations. Resist the temptation! Background sounds might amuse a few shoppers, but they annoy most. You run the risk of turning your prospective customers away immediately without placing a bid.

262. If you are a Trading Assistant, take advantage of the special logo eBay provides you. It makes you look official, and it builds trust in your bidders, whether they contact you to sell for them on consignment or not.

6.

Reaching a Worldwide Market

Because of its very nature as one of the most popular destinations on the World Wide Web, eBay gives you instant exposure to a worldwide audience. But with millions of other individuals selling on the site, many of them offering merchandise that's similar to yours, it's also important to do everything you can to ensure that your sales receive maximum visibility. This chapter explores options for advertising and marketing your sales. You'll also get tips for reaching overseas customers and making it easy for them to purchase from you.

263. Make your items available to an international audience. Provide buyers with prices on several shipping methods to other countries, such as Air Parcel Post and Global Priority Mail.

264. In order to make your items available to the widest possible audience, check the Will Sell to Worldwide box in the Sell Your Item form. But be aware that if you sell overseas, you'll have to do some extra work: you'll have to use special boxes (not the free Priority Mail boxes you might be used to), you'll have to fill out customs forms, and you'll probably have to go to the post office to make sure everything is done right.

265. Whether you fill out eBay's own Sell Your Item form or use software like Turbo Lister to prepare your sales descriptions, make sure your item is specified as being available to overseas buyers. In the Sell Your Item form, you do this on the Enter Payment & Shipping page by checking the box next to Worldwide.

266. You can limit your shipping to specific countries if you want to keep things simple. In the Sell Your Item form, you can uncheck the Worldwide box. Then check the box or boxes next to the countries you do want to ship to—Canada, the United Kingdom, and so on.

267. Avoid slang and obscure references that shoppers whose first language isn't English won't be able to understand.

CUSTOMS AND OVERSEAS SHIPPING

268. Get used to filling out customs forms, and learn which ones are required for different countries. The U.S. Postal Service makes use of a short green form and a white form that asks for more detail. It's hard to know which one to use because the rules vary by destination. If you're waiting in line at the post office, fill both forms out, so you are ready for either one.

269. The white customs form asks how you want to handle an item if it doesn't reach its destination. Do you want the package to be returned to you, at your expense, so you can sell it again? Or should it be treated as abandoned? Give some thought to this beforehand. You don't want to have to make a snap decision while the postal clerk is waiting for you. I've never had a package lost—not yet, at least. I usually specify that they be returned so I can resell them.

270. The My eBay/PayPal/U.S. Postal Service shipping service that makes it easy to print out labels yourself works with international shipments as well as domestic ones. You'll need to have some special plastic sleeves available in which to put the white customs forms. The system tells you which form is required. Make sure you wrap the sleeve and form around the edge of the box so you don't cover up the address.

271. Customs requirements are one reason to use a shipping service like FedEx or UPS. These shippers determine what forms you need and help fill them out for you.

272. When you use the U.S. Postal Service for overseas shipments, be nice to your customers. Be sure to mark your packages as Personal and include an invoice so customs officers in other countries don't open them or charge your customers extra.

273. You also have the opportunity to choose shipping options in the International Shipping area of the Sell Your Item form. The form's drop-down list includes specialized overseas shipping options such as UPS Worldwide Express, UPS Standard to Canada, Standard Int'l Flat Rate Shipping, and many other options.

274. Be sure to check the countries you want to ship to in the International Shipping list. If you don't want to ship to Asia, for instance, make sure that option is unchecked beneath the shipping method you select.

275. There's usually only a few dollars worth of difference between shipping USPS Air Parcel Post and USPS Global Priority Mail. Be sure to give your customers both options.

276. When you are estimating shipping costs to an overseas location, be generous with the figures you give out. Often, packages end up weighing more than you originally thought. It's happened to me: I weighed a pair of shoes in a box and got the weight at about three pounds. I used the USPS shipping calculator (ircalc.usps.gov) and calculated the postage for Air Parcel Post $21.25. I told the customer the shipping cost would be $22.25, adding only $1 for handling. When I did the actual packing and got to the post office, the employee weighed the package and came up with a cost of $23. I not only lost my handling fee, but I lost nearly a dollar on the deal. Always add an extra dollar in case your scale is off.

277. I don't usually offer USPS Economy Parcel Post because it can take four to six weeks, and packages can easily be damaged. If a customer specifically asks for this option, I will provide it, but I will tell the customer about my reservations and let him make the choice.

278. eBay's Sell Your Item form is set up for USPS or UPS options. If you want to use FedEx, DHL, or another service, you need to choose the Other Int'l Shipping option. You'll need to identify the shipper and the options you permit in the body of the auction description.

INCREASING VISIBILITY FOR YOUR EBAY SALES

279. You should be able to locate an item you have for sale in one or two mouse clicks, just like your buyers. Do a test: search for your item using only one or two keywords. Where does it show up in the search results? If it's far down the list, consider adding bold or a subtitle to help it stand out from the crowd.

280. You can evaluate just how many pairs of eyeballs see your description by adding a counter to your listing. Be aware that counters only give you a rough idea of how many people see your sale—they don't tell you how many thought about bidding or planned to bid at some point. They may also slow down the loading of the page on which they appear, so use them only for sales that you really want to track.

281. Speaking of counters, Andale (www.andale.com) gives you the option of adding a hidden counter to your sales when you sign up for their services. A hidden counter is one that only you see—the shoppers who view your description can't tell it's there, so they can't tell they're being tracked.

282. If you sell to a lot of customers in a particular country where you speak the language, consider establishing an eBay Store in that country. You'll gain exposure to even more customers from that market.

283. If you are selling collectibles or antiques that appeal to collectors, find newsgroups where those collectors discuss their passion. Post a message telling them what kinds of items you have for sale. I've seen lots of these messages in newsgroups for fountain pen collectors, for instance.

GOOGLE-BASED MARKETING TOOLS

284. Use Google to attract business to your eBay Store. Google is one of the most exciting sets of web services around. At the very least, you should register your store's name and URL in the Google Web directory (www.google.com/addurl.html) so you can be listed along with other web-based businesses.

285. AdWords is a Google service that works like eBay's own Keywords program. You select keywords related to your store or eBay business. You place a bid stating how much you will pay to have your ad displayed each time someone searches for those keywords. You only pay that amount when someone clicks in the ad. The more you pay, the more often your ad will appear. You can bid between 5 cents and 50 cents per click.

286. Limit your AdWords campaign, especially at the outset, so you don't spend too much on results you haven't tested. You can limit your ads geographically, for instance: target only those parts of the world or areas of the United States where you expect to get the most customers.

287. Limit your ad campaign monetarily as well. You can set a cap that says you won't spend more than $50 or $75 per day on all of your keywords, for instance. While this might not be good for business, it will be good for your pocketbook.

288. You only get ninety-five characters in which to create the text-only ad that will appear on Google search results pages. Pick the most important words you can and pare down your "message" as much as possible.

289. You can also create a blog (an online web-based diary) in which you can talk about your business and collecting activities. You can also place links within the blog to your eBay Store and eBay auctions. The more links you make to your store's home page, the higher your store's ranking in Google search results.

PROMOTING YOURSELF AS A SELLER

290. Create an About Me page. There's no excuse not to have one. It's free, after all. You can use one of the ready-made templates provided by eBay for you. For sellers, an About Me page gives you a chance to promote your experience and your area of interest. You can include a link to your eBay Store, too, and provide a selection of current items for sale.

291. Create a web page for yourself and your business. Chances are your Internet service provider gives you space on one of its web servers where you can post a personal page for no additional cost. Take advantage of this and create a page where visitors can find out more about you. Make a link to your eBay Store, of course.

292. Get a toll-free phone number and include it with each of your auction descriptions. (eBay doesn't let you include a URL in a description, but a phone number is okay.)

293. Email is a terrific tool for getting the word out about your business and your eBay Store. Some enterprising store owners create a mailing list from their customers' email addresses, and periodically send out an email "blast" about their new products and promotions. Each eBay Store owner has the option to create an email list so buyers can find out when new items are listed; go to the eBay Stores home page, click Manage My Store, and log in to find out more about it.

294. You can promote yourself by answering questions and being helpful in eBay's discussion forums. But keep in mind that your current or prospective customers may also be in the audience. Don't forget that workshop comments stay on eBay's site for months at a time, possibly longer, so carefully consider your word choice and watch your language. Your professional reputation as a seller is literally and figuratively on the line.

295. Another discussion forum tip: you've heard of pink slips, but in the case of eBay it's important not to slip up in the presence of a pink, aka an eBay employee. They keep track of how sellers present themselves on eBay forums to make sure you don't include some sort of advertising either in your User ID or in a signature that that is attached to your message. So keep close tabs on what you say and how you present yourself, or you're in danger of receiving a warning message from an eBay moderator.

296. Everything you do as a seller reflects on your professional reputation. That includes your User ID. Try to avoid a User ID that sounds silly or is hard to remember. Don't be in such a hurry that you go with your first instinct. Sleep on it a few nights, and try it out on friends or family members.

297. If, however, you change your mind, it's not a disaster. Remember that you won't lose your feedback or your current auction information if you change your User ID. You only need to go to My eBay, click Accounts, click Change My Personal Information, and then click Change My User ID.

298. Branding is what big-time corporations do to make their company names and slogans household words. Before they could even talk, my kids would beg when we drove past a McDonald's or walked past a Coke machine. Be consistent in your use of color, text, and images.

299. Consider building your own "brand" by coming up with your own logo. You can create your own using a free online utility such as Cool Text (www.cooltext.com), or you can hire a graphic designer and get a high-quality logo for less than $500. You can use it for years to come on your stationery and business cards as well as your web page, so it's well worth the investment.

300. If you've had trouble with nonpaying bidders or if you just want to prevent problems, include a phrase such as this in your descriptions: "Serious bidders only!" or "Don't bid unless you're serious about following through with this transaction." Really, you're doing everyone a favor by not wasting time.

301. One of the best ways to market yourself online is to give something away for free. I'm not talking about giving away your products for nothing. Give away some knowledge—include some tips about your area of interest in your descriptions, on your About Me page, or in a sheet you include with your auction description.

302. If you need a logo or banner ad designed for your eBay business, go to eBay. Look in the Specialty Services category for design services that can help you spread the word. The folks here specialize in designs for the Web, so you won't end up with something that looks good on paper but not so hot on the Web.

BUYING AND MANAGING EBAY KEYWORDS

303. eBay Keywords lets sellers purchase words for a fee; whenever someone searches for one of your chosen keywords, eBay displays an ad with a link to your eBay Store. Who doesn't like the concept of putting forth a little effort up front and then reaping huge benefits without raising a finger?

304. It's not just at school that doing some homework can pay off big. Purchase a few keywords for well-known items, then pause after a week. Wait to see if your sales volume goes up. If so, you should keep purchasing those words. If there is no change, move on to some different words until you find ones that work better.

305. When looking for keywords to buy, be as specific as you can. Instead of "shoe," include a brand, such as "Nike shoe." Since Nike is an important brand, be specific: "Nike TN Trainer," or even "Men's Nike TN Trainer size 11."

306. Along with choosing keywords, you need to create a text box that appears when someone searches for your selected keywords. Give some thought to a word or two, or a phrase, that you can use to advertise your business: try to come up with words that will serve as a "call to action" and that will induce shoppers to click through to your store to find out what you have for sale.

307. Once you achieve PowerSeller status, eBay gives you promotional "dollars" you can spend to promote your keywords. If you're a Bronze level seller, you get a one-time trial credit. PowerSellers at higher levels have a bigger allocation available to them.

308. Don't expect to see your ads appear every time someone, including yourself, searches for them. Your ad space is shared with big companies like Visa and UPS that also take out ads on eBay. This speaks to the need to buy keywords that are very specific so you won't be replaced by sellers with bigger pockets.

309. Here, as elsewhere, it pays to turn to the workshops eBay has held in recent years to get expert tips. The workshop entitled "How to Build Successful eBay Keywords Campaigns" (forums. ebay.com/db2/thread.jspa?ID=410283748) is a good place to start.

Part Two:

During the Sale

7.

Fielding Questions from Customers

When you did your own buying on eBay, you probably asked questions of the people from whom you wanted to buy. You know that the speed with which a response comes and the quality of response directly affect whether or not the person will eventually place a bid. Once you start selling, you're the one who has to respond promptly and courteously, no matter what you're doing. Often, you receive questions that you don't know how to answer. Many times, I've run to my eBay friends for help with responding to tricky questions of one sort of another. In this chapter, I'm happy to return the favor by providing guidance on how to respond to some of the questions I've received.

310. When you are budgeting time for your eBay business, don't underestimate the minutes that turn into hours as you answer any and all questions. It's really important to the community at large as well as to your individual efforts that you respond quickly and thoroughly. I don't think there's any reason for ignoring a question someone sends you—as long as it's an actual question and not a comment.

311. Questions can come at any time, but chances are that the volume will be turned up near the end of a sale. Be ready for questions that come just before a sale closes. Keep track of your schedule and make sure you are at home or near your computer several hours before the sale ends.

312. There is one email from a potential customer to which you don't need to respond. Once in a while, you might get a message from an eBay member who apparently has a lot of time on his or her hands, and who has nothing better to do than to email you to say something like "That thing you're selling sure is ugly," or "Do people really buy these kinds of things?" Don't waste your time responding; no response is better than an angry or irritated comment that might start an email fight.

313. If you end up still owning an object you thought was sold, you still have several good options. You can always relist the item if you cancel the sale; if other bids were placed, you can make a Second Chance Offer to an underbidder.

FIVE WAYS TO MAINTAIN A POSITIVE ATTITUDE

314. Be patient and positive with customers, no matter what complaints they voice. Sometimes they are just having a bad day and need a place to vent. We've all been there. Other times they are confused about the product or don't understand the system. If you can shed a little light on the subject, they will be grateful and calm down immediately.

315. Everyone makes mistakes, whether they are professionals who operate big retail stores or amateurs like you and me. It's easy to get mixed up, no matter how careful you try to be. So don't be too hard on yourself if someone points out a typo or another error in a description. Just pledge to do whatever you can to straighten things out. Chances are your shopper will sympathize with your dilemma and still leave feeling positive about you and your sales efforts.

316. You can learn some really useful things from customers who ask questions. Not only do you discover when you have messed up a description, but you might also learn details that only dedicated collectors know. Once in a while, someone asks if you still have something for sale that went unsold the first time and that you forgot about completely. Take a healthy, positive attitude toward questions; don't look on them as a nuisance.

317. Just because you're using a stock answer doesn't mean you can't be original and personal. Simply put the person's name by the salutation or make a small modification in the text to respond to a special case. Many buyers submit questions with a simple "Hi" or no salutation at all. That doesn't mean you have to do the same. Say "Hello bob4543," or whatever their User ID is.

318. You may be called upon to act as a teacher when you answer a question. Everyone has to start somewhere, and I'll bet you asked plenty of questions when you were new to the game. I know I did. Don't be reluctant to instruct your buyers on basic eBay concepts. You'll save your fellow sellers future questions.

STREAMLINING THE COMMUNICATION PROCESS

319. Create a set of standard email responses so you can save time when responding to questions about things that don't change—such as your shipping and returns policies. There's no need to endlessly keep reinventing the wheel.

320. You don't have to answer questions if you're in the middle of listing or photographing, but make a note of the question and try to get to it by the end of the day. You might designate one hour of the day as "question time." You can use this hour to answer questions, post questions on the discussion boards, or do other eBay-related socializing.

DEALING WITH SPECIAL REQUESTS

321. I once had a question from a shopper in Europe who asked if he could pay by personal check for a $1,500 electronics item. No problem, I said. However, he also asked if I would ship FedEx and insure the item for far less than it was worth. If I would state on the customs form that the item was worth $150, it would save on Europe's high customs fees. I drew the line there, and said no; I don't use FedEx for shipping, and I didn't want to misrepresent the item and risk getting in trouble with customs. You don't have to say yes to everything customers ask; stick to your guns, and you'll probably find someone else who will receive the item.

322. Some buyers have their own preferences when it comes to shipping. I had one buyer go to the trouble of mailing me a shipping label so I could use it, rather than printing out my own label. Why? I have no idea; he may have been charging the shipping to his office. Some buyers feel it gives them more of a measure of control when they do this. If someone insists, provide them with the shipping costs, and let them send you the label.

323. A shipping label is one thing, but what about the buyer who asks if you will use her preferred shipping method? You may be quite used to shipping with the U.S. Postal Service, for example, but a buyer may ask you to use FedEx instead. Only do this if it is convenient for you.

324. Sooner or later, someone will ask you to retract his bid or to undo his purchase. He may have bid without thinking; his son or daughter may have placed the bid without his approval. You'll have to use your judgment when deciding how to respond. Review the user's feedback and see if there have been problems with previous transactions. If it seems like an honest mistake, it's okay to cut him a little slack.

FIELDING THE MOST COMMON QUESTIONS

325. Perhaps the most common question you'll receive is one that only asks you to "confirm" something. The customer asks something you clearly stated in the description. Don't blow these questions off or be impatient with the person. He is probably trying to make sure you're a real seller and that you're reliable and responsive. Just give the answer, thank the person for her interest, and move on.

326. Perhaps the second most common question you are likely to receive is a mistake or discrepancy you made in the description because you were in a hurry and didn't proofread. I'm as guilty of this as anyone. I might say a pair of shoes is size 10 in the title and then 10.5 in the item details, and 11 in the body of the description. Thank the person for pointing out the mistake, and fix it: they're doing you a favor by acting as your proofreader.

327. Questions about the true color of the item you are selling might seem aggravating. But color is unreliable on the Web. It can differ slightly from browser to browser or computer to computer. Take a deep breath and answer the question patiently. Send separate photos on your own as email attachments to reassure shoppers.

328. Sooner or later you'll get a question about dirt, cracks, or other supposed flaws that may appear in your photos. Such marks may not even exist on the actual object, but your buyers may also be using a handheld device to view your options and might have clear images. Don't forget that honesty is always the best policy.

ACTUAL QUESTIONS I HAVE RECEIVED FROM BIDDERS

329. Q: Can I pay for the item using Bidpay [the Western Union payment service] money orders sent to a seller by Western Union? **A:** No problem. Western Union money orders are very secure and reliable; you can treat them like cash.

330. Q: I'm interested in your item, but my PayPal account is not verified because I haven't added a bank account yet. Will you accept a certified check? Thanks! **A:** By all means. Certified checks are a reliable form of payment, though they take some time to clear. Go ahead.

331. Q: I am writing to you about your Allen Edmonds 6.5 D Chelsea shoes that did not sell. This size sometimes is too small for me, but if you will take an offer of $30 including shipping to 70448 I will take my chances. Let me know what you think and I'll get a money order in the mail to you. **A:** Sounds good, let me put the shoes for sale in my eBay Store for $30 and you can purchase them there anytime. **Comment:** This type of question comes up more often than you think. If you sell through your store, you have to pay eBay's fees but you get their buyer and seller protection, too.

332. Q: Would you be willing to ship two- or three-day air? I need to have these for a trip and am in Sacramento. **A:** I usually ship Priority Mail, which delivers in two to five days. There is no guarantee they will get to you in two or three days; however, if you want guaranteed delivery in two days, I can give you a quote for Express Mail.

333. Q: What would be the total shipping cost to zip code 44667 (Ohio) if I buy two or three items from you? **A:** I will be happy to combine shipping and send all the items you purchase in a single package: instead of the $9.99 flat charge for each item, I would charge $10.99 for two items and $12.99 for three.

334. Q: Are you really charging $8.50 for shipping? This hat will ship for $4 maximum through Priority Mail. **A:** Thanks for your inquiry. In fact, the shipping charge was a flat rate that I settled on without actually weighing the item. After weighing and calculating the postage, I see you're correct as long as I ship to your zip code. To other locations the cost would be higher.

335. Q: Do you ship by USPS Economy Surface to overseas/Germany? **A:** I don't recommend this because it can take up to six weeks. Your package can also be damaged in transit. However, if you really want to do this I will give you the cost for this and other options.

336. Q: Are these shoes brown or burgundy? You have several good pictures (which I appreciate), but they look a little more brown than burgundy. A: It's hard to accurately describe the difference between brown and burgundy but they are definitely burgundy. Here's another photo with different lighting so you can look at it again.

337. Q: What is the UK size of these shoes? A: As you know, the sizes of shoes are different in the U.S., and Europe. I only provided the U.S. size; however, the label says the UK size is 6.

338. Q: Will you ship UPS if I send you a prepaid shipping label? A: Yes. **Comment:** This sort of question only comes up rarely but if the customer is willing to pay for shipping and has an account with a shipper, don't say no. Just tell them you want a $1 fee for shipping and handling.

339. Q: Any interest in selling this lamp for $175 right now? If so, I promise I'll follow through and will not back out later, leaving you hanging. I'll pay you immediately, too. A: Sorry, I don't end sales early. Thanks for your interest, though. **Comment:** You often get these sorts of questions with particularly desirable items; if you end the sale early you'll almost certainly lose out on eager bidding that typically comes at the last minute.

340. Q: Would you send a couple of close-up photos of the Harry Cooper iron? I'd like to see face, sole, back of club head. Thanks. **Comment:** If someone is interested enough to ask for more photos of an item (in this case, a golf club), you need to go to the effort to provide them, even if you're busy and the end of the sale is near.

341. Q: If I am the highest bidder, could we use the fastest method of shipping possible, please? I would really like to receive the shoes by July 29th at the latest. Thank you very much. **Comment:** This person wanted a set of golf shoes for a trip she was taking. I did send the shoes by Express Mail, but emphasized that I couldn't guarantee how long they would take to arrive. I shipped them as quickly as I could the morning after the purchase was made. But because she lived in Canada, the customs process added some time to the shipment and she didn't receive them in time. Nevertheless, she was appreciative because I had done the best I could to help her.

342. Q: Is Canada included in the higher shipping rates? **Comment:** Although Canada is close to the U.S. it is indeed a foreign country, and the USPS charges $20 or more for shipments of a few pounds to Canada.

343. Q: If possible, could you send expected time of delivery and tracking number?

Comment: You'll get this question even if you sent an email when the item shipped. Just be patient, look up the tracking number, and send the response. Keep thinking, *Return business . . . I want this person's return business . . .*

LEARNING WHEN TO SAY NO

344. The customer isn't always right. On some occasions, you need to say no. You don't have to waste a lot of time coming up with a big song and dance. Just convey your regrets and simply state your policy. End of discussion.

345. If someone asks you to end a sale so she can purchase an item just a few hours before the auction ends, you need to turn her down, even if she offers you a large amount of money. Your long-term reputation is more important than short-term income.

346. If someone asks to purchase an item using a payment method you don't like, you don't need to accept it. In particular, you should be wary of Western Union wire transfers, which are frequently used by fraudulent buyers.

347. "I'll pay you $XXX if you'll end the sale early and sell it to me right now." Just say no! Sometimes, these offers are quite reasonable. Once in a while, you are offered more than you could sell for otherwise. It doesn't matter: by ending the sale early you make bidders angry, you run the risk of getting negative feedback, and you remove yourself from eBay's safeguards. Completing the transaction is fraught with risk you don't need.

348. As I was writing this, I received an email from someone in the Middle East. He explained that he had glanced at one of my books but had not been able to read it completely because he was very busy. He had an old piece of rock with writing that (he said) was from the ninth century B.C. He wanted me to sell it for him on eBay. There are way too many suspicious and iffy things about such a request. I said no; you should say the same to such requests.

349. For the preceding request, and for all requests to sell something on consignment, you need to make sure of what you're selling. Open the box and closely examine what's inside. Remember that it's you, not the owner, who gets the bad feedback and other repercussions (could the item be stolen, for instance?) if something goes wrong.

350. *Authenticate* is the word you need to write on a sticky note and paste to your computer. Things can get a little awkward if it turns out that an engagement ring that belonged to your ancestor was made of glass instead of a gem. But a fact is a fact no matter how loudly the owner protests that the object is rare and valuable. Don't ever be swayed by emotion and neglect to get an appraisal before putting something online.

351. How soon should you get back to a customer? Try to monitor your email once a day at the very least. It's better to check your mail several times a day. In either case, you should make an effort to get back to customers within twenty-four hours.

VACATIONS AND "DOWNTIME"

352. If you are going on vacation, you can handle eBay listings in a number of ways. Everybody needs to take a break now and then. But on the other hand, how are you going to pay for those airline tickets and resort rooms if you stop selling entirely? Luckily there are ways to deal with the emailed questions you are sure to receive while the sale is ongoing.

353. Here's one way to handle it if you are going to be out of town: in the body of the auction description, state the days you will be out of town, and tell people you simply won't be responding to questions during that period—they should submit questions only before the date you specify.

354. You should plan to be home or in the office when the sale ends. Often, buyers submit instant payment through PayPal. You cannot expect them to wait for you to ship while you are out of town. You should be available to ship within a day or two of the end of the sale. Otherwise, don't start the sale in the first place.

355. If you have an eBay Store, be sure to put your listings on hold while you are out of town. Go to the eBay Stores home page (http://stores.ebay.com), click Manage My Store, and click Store Vacation Settings. Turn vacation settings on. On the Listings and Message Options page, choose an option for how you want to handle your store listings. You can postpone your sales altogether, in which case they won't appear online.

356. If you are on vacation and you have eBay Store listings, you don't have to take your sales offline entirely as described in the preceding tip. Rather, you can add a vacation message to each of your listings. You type the message once in the Listings and Message Options page. Then eBay adds the message automatically to each of your listings during the period while you're out of town.

8.

Revising and Improving Your Descriptions

One of the nice things about publishing on the Web in general, and on eBay in particular, is the ease with which you can revise text. You can—and should—review your descriptions to make sure you haven't made any mistakes. You should also make alterations in response to questions—and complaints—your buyers send you. Don't just leave your descriptions "as is" without trying to improve them. When you relist, look them over to see if there's something you can improve in the title or in the body of the listing. Is there a detail about the condition or color you forgot? Taking the time to make things better and check them over doesn't just make you look professional. It produces bids and purchases, too.

357. You can't always make changes to your descriptions. After a bid has been placed, you can't change the wording, so it's important to be as clear and concise as you can in writing your description in the first place. Print it out and proof it before making it "live," or ask a friend or family member to view it onscreen.

358. Nobody can think of everything. And if you get one question about your sale, chances are there are other potential buyers who are wondering the same thing. Luckily you can answer a question and post the answer along with the listing. That way you're covering all the bases.

359. Even if you can't rewrite your description or make edits because a bid has been placed, you can add to it. If you want to correct something, you can add some explanatory sentences that appear at the end of the description. The new text appears with a time stamp, making it clear that it was added after the auction started.

360. If you are trying to get a group of sales online on a Sunday evening so they'll end at the exact same time the following Sunday, try this trick: prepare your sales descriptions and get them online first. Take photos later and add them as revisions when you have time—either later that night or the following morning.

REVISING CURRENT SALES DESCRIPTIONS

361. Please, double-check your listings after you put them online. As I was writing this book, I checked two pairs of my shoes that didn't sell and that were similar in appearance. I found that I had switched the photos for the shoes. No wonder no one bid on them!

362. If you don't have any bids and it's more than twelve hours before the end of the sale, consider extending the length of the sale. If you started with a five-day sale, change to a seven-day sale; if you started with a seven-day sale, change to a ten-day sale (it's only a 10-cent surcharge). You'll give your item a little more of a chance at being purchased, and you'll avoid having to pay another insertion fee. But remember that after the first bid has been placed, you can no longer change the duration of the sale.

363. What if you were very excited about your item and listed it at a good price, but the silence is deafening? Don't wait until the last minute to discover that your item is doomed to remain yours. Monitor the number of bids on your auction and if you don't like what you see you can add extra features to gain more attention.

364. eBay doesn't let you change shipping instructions after bids have been placed on an item, but you can always use your About Me page to clarify your shipping preferences, provide an address for receiving checks and money orders, and specify which payment services you can accept. You can change your About Me page at any time.

365. eBay's policies with regard to changing current sales descriptions can be confusing. You'll find a rundown of the changes you can make and exactly when you can make them on the Revising Your Listing page at http://pages.ebay.com/help/sell/edit_listing.html.

366. If you have a reserve price, you can change it as long as there are more than twelve hours left in the sale. You can only lower or remove the reserve price, however—you can't raise it. You might want to lower or remove the reserve if you haven't attracted any bids and you want to spark more interest, for example.

367. When it comes to making revisions, you have a lot more freedom with eBay Store listings than you do with auction listings. As long as no item from the listing has been sold (for example, if you have six items for sale in the listing and none have been purchased), at any time while the sale is active, you can change the description or price, add or change photos, and remove optional features. If an item has been sold, you can still revise the price, but you can only add to the description.

368. Before you reply to a question you receive from a prospective buyer, consider posting the question and your answer in the description itself. As long as twelve hours or more are left before the end of the sale, you can do this by checking the appropriate box in the form that eBay sends you in order to compose your response. Some questions and answers are general enough to be of interest to other bidders as well.

369. eBay only lets you revise ten listings at one time. However, if you choose the Edit Listings in Bulk option from My eBay, you can change all of your listings at once—as long as you make the same change to the selling format (such as changing auction sales to Fixed Price sales or eBay Store listings).

FIVE WAYS TO PERK UP HO-HUM DESCRIPTIONS

370. Maybe you need the online equivalent of a neon sign to get more attention for a really special item. You can add bold and highlighting, or change the auction to a Featured listing, for instance. In some cases, presentation really is everything.

371. You might not have thought initially that your item needed a gallery photo, but it's fine to add one in the middle of the stream. Sometimes a picture really is worth a thousand words.

372. You can always add photos to a description—but only if you host the photos yourself. If you host the photos with eBay Picture Services, you can only add photos before the first bid is placed and with more than twelve hours left before the end of the sale.

373. If you're trying to get more attention for your sale, you can list it in a second category anytime up to twelve hours before the sale ends. You can add a category whether or not bids have been placed.

374. One of the best reasons for revising a description is simply to make it more readable. It's good to have lots of details. The more details and sentences you have, the more likely it is that someone will be interested enough to bid. But don't present all the details in a single long block of text. Break it into several shorter paragraphs. Also highlight the most important tidbits by presenting them in the form of a bulleted list. You can create a list with Turbo Lister or the Sell Your Item form, or virtually any eBay auction tool.

RELISTING ITEMS

375. Consider relisting an unsold auction item in an eBay Store. It costs only 2 cents to list there, or 3 cents if you have a gallery photo.

376. If you have made a serious mistake in a listing and eBay's policies prevent you from making changes, your only other option is to cancel the sale. Go to the End My Listing Early form (http://offer.ebay.com/ws/eBayISAPI.dll?Ending MyAuction), log in, and enter the item number. Click Continue, and confirm your choice. You will have to make the changes and relist your item, and pay another insertion fee. However, if your item sells the second time around, eBay will refund your relisting fees.

377. Here's a trick I recently discovered and that I just love. Suppose you want to relist an item but it's no longer in My eBay. My eBay, unfortunately, deletes listings after sixty days. But you don't have to recreate the listing if you search for the item by its title in Completed Items—or, if you retrieve the original email message from eBay stating that the item was not sold, you can open it and click the Relist button. There's a reason for saving all of those messages from eBay after all!

378. If an item doesn't sell the first or second time around, consider changing the auction format. You do this in My eBay. Click the Revise button next to the title of the auction listing. Change the format to Fixed Price. Also check the Best Offer box if you want to receive offers from customers—you'll increase your chances of selling if you do so.

FIVE QUICK AND EASY LISTING UPGRADES

379. If you are able to gift wrap the items you sell, you stand a slightly better chance of making a sale. You can either advertise in the body of your auction description that you will provide this extra level of service, or you can check the Gift Services box and pay an extra 25-cent fee. In return, a gift icon is added to your listing.

380. If you want your listing to stand out from others in a page of search results, one of the most cost-effective options is to make it bold. This makes your auction title appear in bold type, and it only costs an extra $1.

381. You can waste a lot of money on listing upgrades. The fact is that people who shop on eBay are more concerned with titles and subtitles, starting prices, shipping costs, and the like. Don't waste $5 to highlight your listing in a colored band.

382. Featuring your listing in a special section at the top of a set of search results or category listings costs $19.95 or more and should only be used in exceptional circumstances—when you have a very rare or in-demand item to sell. Featuring improves the ranking of your item in search results. The Featured Plus option costs $5 more; it improves not only your search placement but your placement in category listings.

383. One of the most effective and inexpensive ways to gain attention for your item, in my mind, is to add a subtitle. For only 50 cents, you can add some supplementary information about your merchandise that wouldn't fit in the main title. You can add model numbers, colors, or special features that will really grab a shopper's interest.

BASIC HTML TIPS

384. If you need to revise your auction descriptions by accessing them on eBay (through My eBay, for instance), it pays to know some HTML. That's HyperText Markup Language, the set of markup instructions used to format web pages. When you revise a listing, you often have to look at the HTML version. When you see <p>, that's the beginning of a paragraph. When you see </p>, that marks the end of a paragraph.

385. In HTML, line breaks are done in one of two ways. When a paragraph is enclosed by <p> and </p>, the browser adds an extra blank space. If you don't want to add a blank space, you use the <br> command. (A "command" in HTML is called a "tag," by the way. A tag like <p> is a start tag, and one like </p>, with the forward-slash, is an end tag.) Use the <br> command to break a paragraph without skipping a line.

386. If you need to revise the name of a photo and you are forced to look at the HTML commands (this happens frequently to me), look for the <IMG SRC> tag. After this, you'll see a description of where the file is located, followed by the actual file name such as image101.jpg. The part you probably want to change is the image name, not the location. Scroll down to the image's file name using the up, down, left, and right arrow keys on your keyboard, and change the file name to the correct one.

387. If you have formatted some of the text in your description by making it bold or italic, you'll see this designated in the HTML version of your description by the <b> and <i> tags. For example: <b> this is bold text </b>, and <i> this is italic text </i>.

388. If you ever want to center something in your description, use the <center> and </center> tags. The <center> tag goes at the beginning of what you want to center, and </center> goes at the end. You will probably have to use these tags together with the paragraph tags, like this: <p><center> This paragraph is centered on the page. </center> </p>.

389. It's often quite useful to indent a block of text on both the left and right margins. You do this in HTML using the <block-quote> and </blockquote> tags. These work just like the <center> </center> tags. For example: <p><blockquote> This paragraph will be indented on both the left and right. </blockquote> </p>.

390. Hopefully, you won't have to use HTML too much on the Web—unless you want to, of course. If you need to find out more, you can search around the Web for a basic tutorial. There are plenty of HTML primers online. One good one is at Webmonkey: http://www.web monkey.com/webmonkey/authoring/html_basics/.

FIXING PHOTOS

391. Suppose you have incorrectly numbered your photos and your sale has already begun. When you go to My eBay and click Revise Your Listing you discover that you have to wade through an ocean of HTML to find the file names. Try this alternative: rather than changing the numbers on eBay's form, change the numbers on the server where your photos are located.

392. If you don't know how to change file names on your host's server, try this: change them on your computer and upload them to your host with the new numbers.

393. Most photo hosts or web hosting services will give you a user-friendly way to upload and manage files with a web browser. If not, try an FTP application such as WSVFTP or CuteFTP.

394. If your photos don't appear in your auction description, and you don't know why, check their file names. Right click on the broken image icon, choose Copy Image Location, and paste the location into a word processing document. Verify that the URL and file name are exactly correct.

WORKING WITH IMAGE EDITING SOFTWARE

395. What's a good all-purpose image editing program? Ask ten people, and you'll probably get ten answers. Adobe Photoshop is the most powerful image editing program in existence, but it's probably more software than you need. Adobe Photoshop Elements, however, is made especially for editing photos, and is relatively easy for those of us who aren't graphic designers to use. Find out more at the Adobe Systems website at http://www.adobe.com.

396. If your photos turn out to be huge both in file size and physical size, you probably took them at an unnecessarily high resolution, say, 2592 x 1944. You can either retake the images at 640 x 480 or try to change the resolution in an image editor.

397. How, exactly, do you change the resolution of a photo in an image editor? This varies from program to program. In the program I use, Paint Shop Pro by JASC, Inc. (www.jasc.com), open the image. Choose Save As, click Options, and change the DPI to be saved from its current level (300 or 150, for example) to 72. You can also increase the compression level, though this might detract from your image's visual quality. Then click OK.

398. What's the single best "fix" you can make to improve the quality of your photos? Open them in an editor and change the brightness. Too many photos are dark and muddy and cheerless. Simply making your photos brighter will make them more attractive to your viewers.

399. What's the second best way to improve your photos? Crop them. Open them in any editor and click the cropping tool. In almost all cases, this is a rectangle drawn in a dashed outline. Click in one corner of the part of the image you want to save; hold down your mouse button and drag to the opposite corner until you have drawn a rectangle around the part you want to save. Release the mouse button. At this point, you'll probably have to choose a menu option called Crop. The part of the image that is within your rectangle will be saved; the rest will be cut out. Cropping reduces file size and physical size and focuses interest on the object you want to sell.

9.

Tracking Your Sales and Navigating eBay

eBay has been around for ten years now, and it's had plenty of time to create a website so big and complex that simply finding things can be a challenge. In particular, it's a challenge to get a question answered, or to locate a software tool that you heard about somewhere and that's offered for free on the site. Related to this is the challenge of keeping track of the sales you currently have online and the ones that will be ending soon. This chapter explores ways to keep track of your own merchandise for sale on eBay and to find what you want more quickly.

400. Keep a detailed record of what you ship, when it was shipped, and when items have been sold and are awaiting payment. Such a list will come in handy when you can't find something you need to ship out. You'll at least know whether you shipped it out already or whether it's really lost.

401. Print out any invoices that include sales tax. Save all your eBay-related receipts and print out your PayPal records periodically so you have a copy if PayPal goes offline. Then you'll have a paper trail when you need it.

402. Keep your inventory, boxes, and eBay merchandise photographs separate from the rest of your home. Otherwise, it will overwhelm you and your family. Make a work schedule that includes quality time with your loved ones. You'll have more energy when you return to your sales listings.

COMPILING SALES REPORTS

403. Software tools like QuickBooks and Quicken enable you to keep your financial records online so you can access them whenever you want to. A few enterprising eBay sellers have created Excel templates and other record-keeping tools that are specially designed to keep track of eBay expenses.

404. I had been selling on eBay for a long time before I realized I could access reports that eBay compiled about my own sales. eBay Sales Reports are free, but you have to subscribe to receive them. Go to My eBay, log in, and click Subscriptions under My Account. Click the Subscribe link next to Sales Reports.

405. Another report option, Sales Reports Plus, is free if you own an eBay Store. Other users have to pay a monthly fee to use it. The Plus option provides the following data that the other option does not: buyer counts, eBay fees, sales metrics by the ending time, sales metrics by category, and sales metrics by type of sale (fixed price, auction, or store).

406. Once you have subscribed to eBay Sales Reports, you start accumulating them every month. In addition to the report for the current month, you can also view archived reports for previous months. Save them on your computer and back them up onto a hard disk so they don't get lost. You can't depend on eBay to protect them for you.

407. One of the most interesting Sales Reports metrics is the number of repeat buyers you have. If you see repeat buyers who return to your sales over and over again, you should send a newsletter to them with special promotions. They're likely to be interested.

TRACKING YOUR ONGOING SALES

408. Don't get too hung up on the number of shoppers who are watching one of your sales. My eBay not only tells you whether a bid has been placed on one of your items, but it indicates how many people are watching the item. In my experience, the number of watchers is only useful if someone asks you to end the sale early. You can tell them if three, four, or five people have shown an interest in the transaction if you need a reason to say no. Often, items with several watchers go unsold, and those with no watchers end up selling, so you can't draw any big conclusions from your watchers.

409. To Toolbar or not to Toolbar: that is the question. It's convenient to add the eBay Toolbar to your browser's set of default toolbars (as long as your browser is Internet Explorer; the Toolbar doesn't work with Netscape Navigator). The Toolbar lets you search eBay conveniently and helps you watch auctions. However, the way it can track your activities makes some reluctant to install it. Find out more at http://pages.ebay.com/ebay_toolbar.

410. When you're researching sales, you frequently visit pages like the Advanced Search form. When you're listing sales, you revisit the Sell Your Item form over and over. Rather than typing the URL every time you visit one of these pages, add a shortcut to your web browser's Links or Personal Toolbar. Display the toolbar, then copy the URL and drag it directly atop the toolbar to add it to the shortcuts already displayed there.

411. My eBay Summary gives you a snapshot of your sales activity during the past sixty days. It's an important tool for maintaining your PowerSeller status. If your sales drop below $2,000 for the past sixty days, you're in danger of losing your hard-won PowerSeller icon. Step up your sales; eBay will give you a thirty-day review period to get your revenue back up.

412. The Scheduled Items view in My eBay enables you to preview any sales that you've scheduled to start in the future. You can also change the starting and ending times for the sale.

MONITORING EBAY SALES WITH YOUR WIRELESS PHONE

413. If you have a web-enabled cell phone, you can visit the "small screen" version of eBay. On my Cingular service, I connect to the Web, choose Browse Websites, Shopping, and choose eBay. (Alternately, type wap.ebay.com in your phone's mini-browser.) You can view how many people have bid on your sales and what the current high bid price is.

414. The "normal" wireless version of eBay is limited. You only get to view the first twenty or so items for sale. You can subscribe to a more full-featured version of the service on the eBay Wireless website. The Premium service costs $3.99 per month at this writing. Find out more about it at pages.ebay.com/wireless.

415. If you don't have a web-enabled cell phone, you can still track your auctions on your computer. There's no cost to try out a shareware application called eAuction Watcher (www.defoortsoftware.com/ewatcher/index.html). The program lets you track sales on eBay as well as Amazon.com and Yahoo! Auctions.

SIGNING IN AND SIGNING OUT

416. You may not realize it, but eBay has two completely different home pages. Both have the URL www.ebay.com. But if you aren't signed in, you see a simplified page with the heading "New to eBay" at the top. Once you are signed in with your User ID and password, you see the more familiar page with links across the top and left-hand side as well as the bottom of the page.

417. Even if you sign out and then revisit www.ebay.com, you see the usual, familiar page rather than the "New to eBay" page. Why? When you log in, eBay leaves a bit of digital information on your computer called a cookie. The cookie is used to identify you so you don't have to log in so frequently.

418. If you ever forget your User ID, you can sign in using the email address you used to register as an eBay user, but you'll still have to remember your password.

419. You might well ask why you would ever want to sign out once you have signed in. There is a Sign Out link in the set of links that runs across the very top of every eBay page. You might want to sign out so others who use your computer (such as your children) won't start bidding using your User ID.

420. You might also want to sign out so you can sign in with a different User ID. Many users have different User IDs for buying, selling, and posting on the discussion boards.

FINDING YOUR WAY AROUND EBAY

421. There's a very powerful and very easily overlooked link near the top right-hand corner of the eBay home page. It's called Live Help. During weekday working hours, you can click this link and send a message to a real live human being. Use it whenever you get lost on eBay's website.

422. When you come across a web page like eBay's Site Map, which is crammed with links, you could easily spend many minutes looking for a single page you want. Open your browser's Find dialog box by pressing Ctrl+F. Enter a keyword contained in the title of the web page you want. Click Find Next. You may have to click Find Next repeatedly, but you'll find it eventually.

423. Most users, including yours truly, navigate eBay by searching. Once in a while, though, I suggest you browse categories. You'll find a partial list on the left-hand side of the home page. You'll find a more extensive list on the easily overlooked Browse page (pages.ebay.com/buy/index.html).

424. A box called Other Ways to Browse gives you a number of other ways to find what you want on eBay. The link eBay Marketplace Research, for example, lets you subscribe to eBay's in-depth search service. You get access to charts, metrics, and trends on sales prices. A "Fast Pass," at this writing, costs $2.99 for two days. A basic research pass is $9.99 per month, and access to up to ninety days of historical data costs $24.99 per month.

425. There are many other research services, such as Terapeak (http://www.terapeak.com), which provide you with access to eBay search data and other sales data. See chapter 21 for more information on these third-party services.

426. There's a separate stores index page for browsing eBay Stores by category. This page is at http://store-index.ebay.com/custom-front/1.html. It's different than the eBay Stores home page (http://stores.ebay.com), which lets you search stores by keyword as well as browse them.

427. The Common Keywords page (http://keyword-index.ebay.com/a-1.html) gives you yet another way to find items on eBay. It's an alphabetical list of common search terms you can use to find merchandise by brand name.

428. I have a category in which I do the vast majority of my selling: Clothing, Shoes, and Accessories. The category opening page for this category contains some interesting links, including a Clothing Seller's Guide and an Apparel Seller's Newsletter.

429. It's a good idea to bookmark the category page you use the most. You might even want to make it your startup page. The links along the right-hand side change periodically and if you visit from time to time you won't miss anything.

430. If you use Internet Explorer, it's easy to make an eBay category page your startup page. Open the page you want, and copy the URL in the Address box. Choose Internet Options from the Tools menu. On the General tab (which appears by default), paste the URL into the Address box.

431. In Netscape Navigator, choose Preferences from the Edit menu. The Navigator preferences appear by default. Paste the URL into the Location box.

432. If you are paranoid about your privacy, you might want to consider browsing eBay without signing in. Why? eBay tracks your mouse clicks and your movements from page to page through a service called Mediaplex. eBay's Privacy Policy clearly states that they can track a user's computer based on the IP address.

433. There's a set of pages on eBay's site that aren't exactly categories. They're less specific. But if you don't know the exact name of the category you want, you can use them to direct you. They're called Themes, and they give you a different way to "drill down" into eBay's category structure. General themes like Disability Resources, Gadgets & Gizmos, and Country-Western give you a starting point. You'll find them at pages.ebay.com/themes.html.

434. If you ever have trouble finding something on eBay (which happens often, especially in the Help area), use Google. Do a search on Google, but go to the Advanced Search page and make sure you specify that results only come from the domain ebay.com.

435. You know how to track your own sales. Do you want a piece of software that helps you track other sellers? Check out BidSpy (www.licensed4fun.com/bidspy.htm), which reports on the sales activities of competitors you specify.

436. Mpire (www.mpire.com) contains a number of auction management tools. You can search eBay, learn about top searches, and get statistics delivered to your cell phone with the ResearcherMobile product.

Part Three:

After the Sale

10.

Ins and Outs of Online Payments

Getting paid for items purchased on the Internet is one of the most important—and potentially nerve-racking—processes for both buyer and seller. But as a seller, you do have an advantage. It's the buyer who has to meet your terms of payment. The buyer also has to give up his money and wait to receive what has been purchased. If you are clear about your payment methods and use electronic systems like PayPal or money order services like BidPay, you'll encounter few, if any, problems. The tips presented in this chapter will streamline the payment process and ensure that you get what you need (the money) so your customers can get what they need (your merchandise) as efficiently as possible.

437. Checkout is the name given to eBay's automated payment service. It's the service that sends an invoice automatically to a buyer when an item is purchased. You can specify in the Sell Your Item form or Turbo Lister that you prefer to send your own customized invoices if that is really important to you. I've never had problems with Checkout; it gives me one less thing to worry about as a seller, and that makes me happy.

USING MY EBAY TO TRACK PAYMENTS

438. When an item has been sold, go to My eBay. Once the buyer has either paid through PayPal or indicated that a payment is forthcoming, a figure will appear in the Total Price column next to the Sale Price. Click on this price to get the payment details. You'll either see that the item has been paid for through PayPal, or that the buyer is going to pay by check, money order, or eCheck.

439. When you click Total Price in the Items I've Sold view of My eBay, you go to the Seller's Payment Status page. You can perform many useful functions from this page. You can contact the buyer, mark the item as shipped, mark it as payment received, sell a similar item, or leave feedback.

440. You can get even more information about a payment by choosing View Payment Details from the drop-down list in My eBay. The Seller's Payment Status page appears. But once payment has been made, an additional option appears: View PayPal Payment for this item. Click it, and log in.

441. When you choose View PayPal Payment from the drop-down list in My eBay, you go to the Transaction Details page in PayPal. This page tells you the ID number for the eBay payment—which can come in handy in a dispute. You get the exact time the payment was made, and confirm that PayPal actually received and processed the payment.

USING PAYPAL TO RECEIVE PAYMENTS

442. There's a reason why PayPal appears in so many eBay auctions. It's eBay's own payment system. PayPal began as an independent payment service that grew to be more popular and far more reliable than eBay's own electronic payment service. So eBay bought the company. Once you start selling on eBay, does that mean you need to automatically sign up to accept payments via PayPal? No, you aren't obligated to use PayPal.

443. Some sellers who have had problems getting issues resolved with PayPal refuse to use the system; they accept checks and money orders from the post office or payment services like BidPay. But if you're just starting out, it makes sense to sign up with PayPal because it's so convenient, it's so tightly integrated with eBay and the U.S. Postal Service, and because the majority of users never run into serious problems with it.

444. PayPal is a fast and convenient way to receive payment, but it's also costly. I'm being charged 2.9 percent plus 30 cents per transaction simply to receive payments. When I sold a piece of electronic equipment for $1,500, the buyer offered me the choice of a personal check or PayPal. Normally, I'd choose PayPal for convenience and speed. But PayPal's fee would have been $48 to receive that large a payment, and I chose the check instead.

445. The Transaction Details page in PayPal gives you some essential details about the buyer. When you scroll down to the Shipping Address area, you not only get the address, but the buyer's name, User ID, and real email address. The email address can help you if you need to provide a refund, or if you want to contact the buyer outside of eBay's message system.

446. An eCheck payment occurs when a PayPal customer does not pay with a credit card, but makes a debit withdrawal from a checking account. PayPal treats eCheck payments just like checks: they take two or three days to be credited to your account.

447. PayPal's account system is similar to most checking accounts in one aggravating aspect: when a debit is made to your account (such as a payment you make with your PayPal debit card), it is deducted from your balance almost immediately. But credits to your account can take days to be recorded.

448. Apply for a PayPal debit card, and you can earn interest on purchases you make when you use the card as a credit card (you can use the card either way). The debit card gives you a convenient way to spend the "fun money" you make through eBay. You can also use it to purchase postage for eBay-related shipping, and purchase inventory you can sell on eBay.

449. Be sure to verify your PayPal account so you look more trustworthy to prospective buyers. It's easy, and it's one of those things that buyers only notice if you don't do it. If you're listed as "Unverified," they might wonder whether you're just lazy and haven't verified, or whether you are untrustworthy.

450. PayPal sellers' accounts come in three different varieties: Personal, Premier, and Business. Chances are you want to sign up for the Premier account. It costs a little more than the Personal account in that PayPal takes a little higher percentage out of each payment you receive. But Personal only allows you to send money to another member. As a seller, the big advantage of using PayPal is that you enable buyers to pay you using their credit or debit cards. You can do so either with a Premier or Business account.

451. If your company (or your home-based business) sells through eBay and you need to give more than one person access to your account, choose a PayPal Business account. Fees are the same as for a Premier account; the main difference is that you have multi-user access to your account.

452. You've probably seen the "PP" logo next to eBay listings on which PayPal is accepted. This logo appears so much that it's probably overused. But it's free, and it might tell a few newbies (new users) that you're a PayPal merchant. (In fact, the overwhelming majority of eBay sellers accept PayPal.) Once you become a PayPal merchant, you have to tell the service that you want to automatically add the logo to your listings. Log in to PayPal, click Auction Tools, and click the link Offer PayPal on All Your Listings (Automatic Logo Insertion).

453. One of the easiest ways to earn a little extra money is to let your buyers know you prefer PayPal as your method of payment. You add an extra phrase "This Seller Prefers PayPal" to all your listings. If you do, you earn 1 percent cash back on every purchase you make with your PayPal credit card. Log in to PayPal, click Auction Tools, and click PayPal Preferred to find out more.

454. Make sure you associate a credit card to your PayPal account. This enables you to become a Verified PayPal member. Just as important, it enables you to transfer the payments you receive to your checking account when you need to.

455. Remember that not all PayPal payments are instant. If the buyer deducts his PayPal payment amount from his credit or debit card, you receive the payment immediately. However, the buyer can also pay by eCheck. An eCheck payment works like a transfer from one checking account to another. PayPal will also notify you if the buyer has indicated that she will pay by check or money order. In that case only the notification comes from PayPal; you have to wait for the payment to arrive in the snail mail.

456. If you receive a notification from PayPal that a buyer will pay you by eCheck, don't ship immediately. It does take several days for the eCheck to clear. Wait for the notification from PayPal that the eCheck payment has cleared before you ship.

OTHER FORMS OF PAYMENT

457. Besides PayPal, be sure you tell shoppers that you accept checks and money orders, which are very reliable forms of payment. Also consider accepting Western Union BidPay money orders (www.bidpay.com).

458. Should you accept personal checks? I've never had a problem with them. Most sellers state in their auction description that they'll deposit the check and wait seven to ten days until the check clears—until the payment is actually credited to their account—before they ship. In practice, you never really know for sure if a check is going to bounce or not.

459. Cashier's checks are a little safer than personal checks because the amount is immediately deducted from the buyer's checking account before the check is actually issued. But they usually carry a fee, so buyers don't like them as much as personal checks. You should certainly state that you accept them, however.

460. Postal money orders are inexpensive to obtain and a very secure form of payment. You should definitely offer them as a payment option to your customers. I've received money orders that weren't signed; it's possible the buyers didn't know they had to be signed. If you get one without a signature, send it back and ask the buyer to sign it.

461. The U.S. Post Office is the most economical source for money orders, but it's not the only source. Don't be surprised if you receive money orders from Payingfast.com (www.payingfast.com), which provides them as well.

462. Another well known money order service is Payko (www.payko.com) . It issues TravelersExpress money orders and it is comparable in cost to Payingfast.com.

463. Should you accept cash? I've said no in several books I've written. Then, one day, I encountered a buyer who insisted on sending actual money in an envelope and who claimed he had never encountered problems. I said okay, crossed my fingers, and everything worked out fine. If you get a buyer who insists on cash, consider bending the rules and accepting it to keep the person happy. You don't have to ship until the money arrives, anyway.

464. Should you accept credit cards? Definitely, but only under two circumstances. If you run a business and you already have a merchant account, use it to process electronic payments. If you don't, your customers can pay with their credit or debit cards through a payment service such as PayPal.

465. What about BidPay, the Western Union payment service? It's very secure and a good alternative to PayPal. What's more, BidPay puts the burden on buyers to pay a fee to obtain the money order. You, the seller, don't have to pay a fee to accept payment, the way you do with PayPal. Definitely sign up for this service.

466. What about Western Union wire payments? Once again, the conventional wisdom says no. These are risky and frequently used by fraud artists who try to trick sellers. But I once had a buyer in the Ukraine who insisted on it and seemed trustworthy, and it worked out fine. The only trouble was that I had to go to the local currency exchange to pick up the payment. Only do this if buyers have a substantial amount of positive feedback.

467. One common scam involving Western Union wire transfers: the buyer says he can't pay the $1,000 for some reason, but if you wire transfer $2,000 to him, he'll pay it all back to you. Don't believe it!

468. What if the buyer offers to wire transfer payment directly to your checking account? I've never done this on eBay, but I have accepted such payments for writing books. The only trouble is that you need to keep monitoring your account to make sure the payment has actually arrived. Other than that, I can't think of any reason to say no.

469. Are there any buyers from whom you should not accept payment of any sort under any circumstances? Some sellers go to the trouble of stating in their descriptions that they won't accept bids from anyone who is designated by eBay as a nonpaying bidder (NPB) or someone who has a negative feedback rating. Usually, they only add such statements after they have been burned by one of those individuals. It's definitely optional, but you can add such a statement to your Terms of Sale if you want to be protected. Personally, I think such statements turn bidders away because they sound too negative.

470. Draw up a schedule for pursuing nonpaying bidders. Use standard, businesslike email templates, and follow eBay's procedure for resolving disputes. Don't let communications get personal.

471. If you sell to someone in Europe, you might receive a request to use the payment service Moneybookers.com. This service makes it easy for European users to convert euros to other currencies. It's a reputable service, but if you don't want to go through the trouble of signing up for Moneybookers.com just to receive one payment, don't do it. European buyers can pay via PayPal just like domestic buyers. Specify in your listings that PayPal is your preferred method of payment, and your buyers will get the message. You become a "PayPal preferred buyer" through PayPal itself. Log in to PayPal, and on the My Account page, click PayPal Preferred under the heading Enhance Account.

472. Thankfully, the Sell Your Item form no longer contains an option for C.O.D. (Cash on Delivery). I don't recommend it as a form of payment. It puts the responsibility on the delivery person to collect your money at the time of delivery. Trust PayPal or another payment service instead.

MERCHANT ACCOUNTS

473. Suppose you want to go beyond PayPal and electronic payments. You want to sell through a brick-and-mortar drop-off store, and you want the ability to process actual credit cards that are handed to you. Your first step is to apply to a bank or specialized merchant account service for a merchant account.

474. When you apply to a financial institution for a traditional merchant account, expect to pay an application fee of $300 or more. Also, have detailed financial information ready, including the amount of your average transaction, your largest expected transaction, the annual sales volume in credit card sales you expect to conduct, and how and where you plan to advertise.

475. Once you get a merchant account, you need a way to process credit card numbers. You either have to buy or rent a hardware terminal of the sort you see in almost every retail store, or software such as that provided by iAuthorizer (www.iauthorizer.com).

476. If you obtain a traditional merchant account, expect to pay lots of fees. These include a per transaction fee (10–30 cents), which the financial institution charges you each time you sell something. You are also charged a monthly fee ($30–$70) to maintain the account, and a "discount rate" or service fee of 1 to 4 percent per transaction.

477. As an alternative to a traditional merchant account, you may want to contact a company that specializes in providing merchant accounts to Internet sellers. These include Merchant's Choice Card Services (www.merchantschoice.com) and 1st American Card Service (www.1stamericancardservice.com).

478. If you want to avoid merchant accounts and PayPal, try a service like ProPay, which is designed especially for online business. You pay a $35 annual fee and a 3.5 percent fee plus 35 cents for each transaction.

11.

Packing

The key to a successful transaction is getting your merchandise to your customers quickly and in good shape. Good packing is essential to every eBay transaction. However, it's a process that's overlooked by many sellers—that is, until they have to start packing up what they've sold. You realize very quickly that packing is a time-consuming process that can be physically demanding and that requires time and attention to detail. If you rush through packing, you not only run the risk of damaging an item, but you could easily mix up packages and shipping labels and end up with a complicated set of problems to resolve. (I know; it's happened to me.) This chapter presents tips for simplifying the process of packing up your merchandise so it's as economical and streamlined as possible.

479. We all love that excited feeling of satisfaction after we complete our first few sales on eBay. But there's also an uh-oh moment when you discover a hidden challenge you hadn't fully anticipated: shipping. Make sure before you even begin to put an item up for sale that you figure out exactly how you're going to ship it and how much that's going to cost. In some cases, the difficulties you would face at the final stage of selling a particular item might make you think twice about getting the process started at all.

480. Have you ever noticed that the attractively wrapped gift gets picked first at the annual office grab bag? When you're selling on eBay, your careful packaging isn't just window dressing. For one thing, it says that you care and reflects well on your professionalism. But more than being a courtesy, it prevents unhappy buyers from complaining about the condition of their purchase.

481. You've probably heard sage advice from home repair experts about "measuring twice and cutting once" before you cut a piece of wood or drywall. Keep your tape measure handy for providing the height, width, and depth of bulky items. In fact, it might be worth your while to invest in a heavy-duty, industrial-strength measuring device. Metric might also be useful at times.

482. What's the difference between "full service" and "average service"? Some shippers want the item to be put in a convenient location where it can easily be loaded onto a truck. Others will save you the heavy lifting by going into your basement or anywhere else your object is stored. Of course, you'll pay extra for the full-service option that includes carrying and loading.

483. Another task when you're putting an item up for sale is to estimate its weight, which will give you a good idea of how much it will cost to ship. To add a calculator to your auctions with Freightquote.com, for example, you need to sign up for a free account. They have eighteen different categories of items.

484. Don't be penny-wise and pound-foolish when it comes to packing. Go ahead and pay a little extra for a padded envelope instead of a flat one and for a corrugated box instead of just plain cardboard. Getting more cushioning to protect your merchandise is worth it.

485. Hopefully what happens to your package on the way to your buyer won't be anything like what happened to the livestock in the Union Stock Yards in Chicago as described in Upton Sinclair's *The Jungle*, but it's better to be safe than sorry when it comes to packing. When in doubt, throw on a few more protective layers of paper, packing peanuts, or bubble wrap.

486. My eBay is integrated with PayPal and the USPS; use the service to print your own shipping labels and calculate your own postage.

TAPE AND OTHER ACCESSORIES

487. If you need to weigh an object, your first challenge is to find a floor scale that will hold potentially hundreds of pounds. Getting the object on the scale might require you to find a piece of plywood that is slightly larger than the object and then put the object on the plywood to distribute the weight evenly. You'll probably need several people to do the heavy lifting.

488. If your buyer is more anxious about money than time, uShip's online directory of shippers includes companies that will pick your item up only when they already have a nearly full load on their truck. You'll incur a lower shipping cost if the run to your buyer is included with their other deliveries.

489. If you're like me, you have a whole drawer full of half-used rolls of tape, so you're probably not going to be happy when I tell you to leave your leftovers in the drawer. Take my advice and invest in pressure-sensitive plastic or nylon-reinforced tape. Or go for water-activated paper tape that is sixty-pound grade and at least three inches wide.

490. Sometimes I use short but strong lengths of tape in order to hold down the loose edges of bubble wrap or packing paper. The U.S. Postal Service offers rolls of free Priority Mail stickers that fill this purpose perfectly. And did I mention that they're free?

491. Your Aunt Lulu was so excited at your last birthday party to give you a desk accessory set that included a panda bear with a place for a roll of tape to fit into his body and a mechanism so his teeth would chop off pieces of tape. Sorry, Lulu, but Mr. Bear had better move over for a handheld dispenser that will make your packing go more quickly. In fact, pacifist or not, you might want to start packing a piece by investing in a tape gun.

492. Speaking of labels, all your efforts will be for naught if both your return address and the intended destination of your package come out in the wash. Roofs can leak on both trucks and warehouses, floods happen, and some packages are even stranded on a porch in the midst of a torrential downpour. Use waterproof ink on a quality label to begin with. Then cover the label with clear tape or use one of those window envelopes—maybe both.

493. Be sure to include a duplicate invoice or label inside your box. That way it can still get to its destination even if the outer label is somehow lost. When you ship overseas, customs officials require an invoice inside the box.

494. Take a look at the maximum gross weight capacity of the box. It's usually printed on the bottom. (Did you ever notice it?) Make sure you don't fill the box with more than it can handle.

PACKING MATERIALS

495. Your focus may wisely be on preventing breaking and smashing, yet water damage is also a worry. Garbage bags are for holding more than garbage. Chances are you can find the perfect size to enclose your item. Before you secure it all with tape, put an extra label on the inside just for good measure.

496. Finding recycled packing material can save you lots of money. Ask your friends and coworkers to save any bubble wrap and packing peanuts they find. Pre-used boxes are fine as long as they are in exceptionally good shape. Use Priority Mail so you can order the USPS's free boxes and have them delivered to your door.

497. In my city, Chicago, April 1 and October 1 are known as especially heavy moving days. All the scavengers who scour the alleys for goodies (including me) make sure to go out the next day. You'll find plenty of bubble wrap and packing material.

498. It's amazing how many people throw out bubble wrap and packing peanuts. You can save tons of money by strolling the alleys and picking up such materials, as long as they're clean and dry. You'll be keeping those materials out of the landfills by recycling them, too. Look for boxes from Pottery Barn, Crate and Barrel, and other well-known outlets, which tend to use lots of good packing materials.

499. In the good old days, the U.S. Postal Service gave out free Priority Mail packing tape. Those days are long gone. Don't pay $2.50 to $3 or more for a roll of packing tape. Go to a dollar store and ask if they have it. I've been able to find rolls of tape for $1 each. I hope you can, too. eBay itself is a great source for tape, bubble wrap, and packing peanuts for sellers. Go to http://search.ebay.com/bubble-wrap and you'll find lots of possibilities as well as links to related searches for packing tape and other materials.

500. This might seem obvious, but if you are packing porcelain, pottery, glass, or other fragile items, pack them individually. Put enough packing material around each so that they are separated from one another.

501. If you ship electronics equipment and some of the connectors, jacks, or other components are exposed, make sure you use anti-static packing materials. That way you won't run the risk of static electricity that can severely damage the device.

502. If you are shipping valuable coins or jewelry, pack them so they don't rattle. Consider using a box that is purposely big so people don't get the idea that small valuables are inside.

503. If you are shipping artwork, don't use contact paper, corrugated paper, or other scratchy materials. They could damage the valuable items.

EIGHT TIPS FOR USING BOXES

504. When you're scrounging for packing material you can use, keep an eye out for high-quality boxes from moving companies. These are especially strong and well-made and really should be re-used rather than thrown in the landfill.

505. Be sure to tape the edges of your box along the bottom, not just the seam that goes down the middle. A little bit of rein-forcement will prevent the box from falling apart. It's especially important to reinforce the edges if you are recycling a used box.

506. When you pack frequently for eBay, you learn about all different types of boxes. The ones with ridges in between two layers of paper are called corrugated boxes. These are the Rolls-Royce of boxes because they're so strong. If you can find them economically, use them.

507. Use your shipping box to do some marketing. Include your business card and an information sheet containing details about you or your business—or, better yet, a reminder to visit your eBay Store.

508. Don't throw away those used boxes you don't need right away. Pile them up in your work area so you have them when needed. Customers don't care if your boxes are used as long as their merchandise arrives quickly and is well-packed.

509. In some cases, it's a good idea to double pack, so try to find boxes that nest into each other. That way it really doesn't matter if the inner box is a little marked up, as long as it's clean.

510. If you have an item that's long and thin, such as a tennis racket, it won't fit in a single Priority Mail box. However, you can take two boxes that are approximately three inches deep by fifteen inches long and tape them together. This makes one box that's three inches deep and up to twenty-nine or thirty inches long.

511. Let the post office do the work. Open up an account and order some free Priority Mail boxes from the USPS Store (www.usps.gov). You'll find some sizes online that you can't get at your local post office. (I like box #7 for packing shoes.) They're free—I repeat, free—and you can have them delivered right to your front door.

MISCELLANEOUS PACKING TIPS

512. Packing is the ideal task for a teenager to handle. If you need help, put an ad up at the local high school; a high school student can come in the afternoon several times a week and help you get packages out the door before the last postal pickup of the day.

513. If you use calculated shipping costs with your auctions, be sure to write down the weight of the package. eBay's shipping calculator doesn't work with buyers in overseas countries. If they're interested in what you have to sell, they'll email you and ask for the cost. Having the weight written down somewhere will keep you from having to re-weigh the item (which I've had to do several times).

514. Buy some inexpensive gift items you can give away with each of the products you pack. If you sell shoes, you might include a pair of new laces, for instance. A business card, photo, or other item personalizes the sale and is sure to impress your customers.

515. As I write this, I'm receiving emails from a buyer who is asking me to ship with a service I don't normally use, to value the item a certain way, and to double pack the item as well. It's testing my patience. Yet I'm going to take a deep breath and try to leave the person satisfied; I'm going to wait a day or so until my irritation subsides. If you run into a demanding person, I suggest you do the same.

516. Often, I have a large number of boxes to pack and ship out on Monday afternoons. This is because most of my sales end on Sunday nights. I sometimes assemble and tape boxes the day before; it gives me one less thing to do on shipping day.

517. One of eBay's own Reviews & Guides pages (search.reviews.ebay.com/Shipping-Charges) is devoted to shipping. Specifically, you'll find tips and instructions designed to purchase postal scales and related hardware wisely.

518. Be sure to stuff paper into anything that is flexible and can be crushed or misshapen. Your customers expect it. I always stuff my shoes full of newspaper, for instance, so they maintain their shape while in transit.

519. Some people love to chop down their own Christmas tree and pick their own strawberries ripe from the patch, so don't rule out the possibility of specifying "Pickup Only." You list the item on eBay and tell buyers you're not going to ship at all. Rather, they have to come to you. They can pay you either electronically or in person. But the important thing is that they assume responsibility for moving. Of course, this pretty much restricts you to prospective buyers who are either local or really, really motivated.

520. Usually it's up to the buyer to purchase insurance. But, to protect your investment, you might want to consider paying a few dollars to ship something really precious and expensive, even if your buyer doesn't want to.

12.

Postage and Shipping Charges

Postage and shipping charges are an inescapable part of selling on eBay. Your job is to find a shipping service and a system that you can work with and that doesn't seem excessively expensive to either you or your customers. You can easily end up spending money and possibly even losing revenue if you "misunderestimate" shipping costs or weights. And you can make things more expensive for your customers if you don't include the proper paperwork when needed, or if you don't meet size and weight restrictions. This chapter presents basic tips for calculating postage accurately and keeping shipping charges down to a manageable level.

521. You'll keep shipping costs down if you use innovative packing materials. Any packing materials that use air for cushioning will be great for your eBay shipments. Amazon.com typically uses big air-filled cushions in the packages they send out; they can easily be re-purposed by you. Remember, packing materials need to be clean and dry, not necessarily new.

522. For items like single postcards or photos that weigh less than eleven ounces, Priority Mail is overkill, especially if the buyer lives in a state near you. Offer First Class mail as an option, and you'll make the buyer happy and save her some money.

523. All of those grocery store plastic bags cluttering up your shelves can be bundled up and used as packing material, too. You can even use several bags to wrap up a book, put it in an envelope, and send it Media Mail economically and safely.

524. Print out your own postage through PayPal or through a service like Click 'n' Ship. Ask your local post office if deliveries of packages that have postage affixed can be made through the back door. You won't have to wait in long lines.

FINDING A POSTAL SCALE

525. Invest in an accurate digital postal scale. Misestimating postage can cause packages to be returned. Worse, your customers might be asked to make up the difference, resulting in great embarrassment.

526. Some postal scales are preprogrammed with postage rate information. Others can download current postal rates from the Internet. Maybe I'm old-fashioned, but I don't think you should pay extra for this. We all know how frequently rates change. Plus, if you use My eBay and the U.S. Postal Service, your postage is calculated for you automatically.

527. Having criticized the automatic postal rate feature in the previous tip, I have to mention another high-tech feature, postage rate comparison, that is worthwhile. If you can afford a high-end postal scale that does comparison shopping, it will actually suggest the most economical rate. Not only that, but some models do compare postage rates between the USPS and other carriers like DHL, FedEx, and UPS. If you can find a model that does all this and it's in your price range, consider it worth the expense. The best place to find such scales is, of course, eBay; just do a search for "postal scale" and you'll find lots of possibilities.

528. If you're looking for high-end, business-oriented postal scales, shop through many different categories. The Business & Industrial category might carry a full-featured model that can handle a lot of weight.

529. Make sure you pay extra for a scale that will handle a sufficient amount of weight. Don't scrimp on a cheap one that only goes up to, say, two pounds, and then have to go to the post office to weigh the item.

530. For really heavy packages, I use my home scale—the same one I use when I desperately try to see if I've lost weight. I have a high-quality doctor's office–type scale rather one that uses a spring. Pay extra for this type of scale and you'll get double duty out of it.

THE GOOD OL' U.S. POSTAL SERVICE

531. The U.S. Postal Service offers Priority Mail Flat Rate boxes, which are good under certain circumstances. Specifically, the item you ship has to fit in the box, and it needs to be really heavy. Then the flat rate postage charge is worth it. For an item that only weighs a pound or two, you'll save money for your customer by shipping regular Priority Mail.

532. Unfortunately, you can't cover up the words "Flat Rate" on the outside of one of the flat rate boxes or envelopes. You also can't extend the size of the boxes the way you can with regular Priority Mail boxes. You have to use them in their original size or not at all.

533. The real problem with Priority Mail Flat Rate boxes is that they are so small. They're far smaller than regular Priority Mail boxes. For me, they don't work, because I can't put a pair of shoes in them. Once, I sold a ten-pound Bible, and it fit perfectly in one of the flat rate boxes, so it paid off well. Otherwise, you have to use the bigger Priority Mail boxes, which aren't flat rate.

534. Be sure you know about size restrictions imposed by the U.S. Postal Service. There's a big difference in postage between an "Envelope/Package" and a "Large Package." If you ship overseas using Global Priority, the box you use is limited in size.

535. Express Mail seems expensive and excessive. But if you offer it, your item is listed as a Get It Fast option. Buyers who check this option in the Search Options box on the left side of a search results page will see it listed. You might just get more business by offering it.

536. Keep in mind that Express Mail, like Priority Mail, comes with its own containers, which you can pick up for free from the post office. You can also order them online from the Postal Store (http://shop.usps.gov).

537. If you have something really expensive and precious to ship, consider Registered Mail, which is the most secure form of shipment. Use it for airline tickets, antique papers, rare antiques, and collectibles.

SHIPPING AND HANDLING CHARGES

538. No less an authority than the UC Berkeley Haas School of Business reports that eBay sellers can increase profits by setting a low opening bid and setting higher shipping charges. The lower starting bid attracts more bidders. The purchaser is not likely to complain about high shipping charges.

539. A totally different school of thought charges higher initial prices but offers free shipping. Which is best? Personally, I don't subscribe to either of these schools. I charge a fixed price for shipping shoes ($9.99) and use the calculator for everything else. I try to make a dollar or two on shipping. I try to set my starting price so I make at least $10 on each sale. It's not a bad idea to experiment with free shipping or low starting prices, though, to see what happens.

540. Deduct your shipping charges from your PayPal account. I like to keep my eBay income and expenses separate from other debits and credits. If you ship using My eBay and PayPal, as I do, you automatically deduct postage charges from your PayPal account when you print out your shipping labels. The system is set up to link the USPS charges and PayPal.

541. A reasonable handling fee is $1. You add this to the shipping cost when you calculate shipping in Turbo Lister or on the Sell Your Item form. Don't gouge buyers by trying to eke out additional profits with higher handling fees. They can calculate postage for themselves and determine if they've been overcharged, and they just might complain about it.

542. A flat shipping fee will make your life simpler if you sell lots of items that are basically the same size and weight. Rather than having to weigh each item and calculate postage separately, you just add the flat fee. For shoes, I charge $9.99 for shipping. On some lightweight models, I'll charge $9 or $9.50. Most of the time, the actual shipping cost is less.

543. If you don't use a flat shipping fee, make sure you use eBay's shipping calculator when you create your auction description. The calculator includes a provision for a handling fee. And it gives shoppers the feeling that they're in control, which increases the likelihood that they'll make a purchase.

544. eBay's shipping calculator only works with the U.S. Postal Service and United Parcel Service (UPS). What if you want to provide your buyers with a shipping calculator and you use FedEx, DHL, or another shipper? Look into the Zonalyzer (http://www.zonalyzer.com), which lets you embed a calculator to a web page or an auction listing.

SHIPPING ON HALF.COM

545. Half.com (half.ebay.com) is eBay's marketplace for low-priced books, CDs, DVD, and other household goods. If you find the shipping procedures on the regular part of eBay too complicated, sell here. Often, you don't need to take photos; Half.com inserts them automatically as long as you have an ISBN or other product number. Half.com requires that you ship by USPS Media Mail or expedited shipping and gives you a standard allotment for shipping that is passed on to the buyer—$3.70 for a hardcover book, for instance.

546. Half.com only works with the U.S. Postal Service. If you prefer UPS or another shipper, you'd better sell on the regular part of eBay.

547. One of the problems with Half.com is that you're not in control of specifying the shipping method. It's up to the buyer to decide whether to use Media Mail or expedited shipping such as U.S. Priority Mail. If the buyer uses Media Mail, the item can take weeks to arrive, and you are likely to receive complaints. It's a good idea to make this clear to the buyer beforehand.

UPS SHIPPING CHARGES

548. eBay definitely favors the U.S. Postal Service, if only because it's integrated with My eBay. But eBay also has a UPS Service Center (www.servicecenter.ups.com/ebay/ebay.html). You can go here if you need to track a package you've sent with them.

549. I've heard of sellers who have an account with UPS and who schedule regular pickups. Every day, they simply leave their boxes in their front yard and the driver picks them up at the appointed time. UPS charges 60 cents or so per package for a truck stopping fee, but this cost is added to shipping charges.

550. Some sellers use UPS's own bar code software to label the packages; the driver only has to scan them and cart them away. You can get the software on the UPS website (www.ups.com).

MISCELLANEOUS SHIPPING TIPS

551. You should try to ship out within a day or two of receiving payment. You are required by law to notify the buyer, telling him when you will ship, if you can't ship within thirty days of payment (for instance, if you don't have the object on hand and you are using a drop-shipper).

552. It's obviously good business practice to ship what someone has purchased, and not to overcharge your customers. If someone complains about being overcharged or not receiving what he purchased, and the complaint is made in writing within sixty days of the purchase, don't ignore it—even if you didn't do anything wrong and did ship the merchandise on time. The Fair Credit Billing Act requires that your customer has the right to complain to you in writing, and you, in turn, are required to respond in writing and then resolve the complaint within ninety days. The obvious ways to remedy the situation are either by shipping the item or providing a refund, or tracing a lost package and applying for a refund to the post office.

553. Get a PayPal debit card. They're free and you can use them at the post office to buy stamps or pay for overseas shipments or other shipments you make in person. You can also use this card to purchase inventory. When you use this card as a credit card the purchase price is deducted from your PayPal account; there are no finance charges, and you earn interest on each credit card purchase, to boot.

554. If you ship heavy items like motorcycles or riding lawn mowers, and you need shipment from a carrier like Roadway, go to http://www.freightquote.com to get an estimate.

555. Don't sweat the small stuff when it comes to postal charges. Occasionally, I am charged more than $10 to ship shoes to the West Coast or another location on the perimeter of the U.S. Not only do I not get my handling fee, but I take a loss on shipping for that particular item. I don't complain, though. On most items I make a few dollars profit in shipping and handling, which makes up for the occasional miscalculation.

556. Consider giving a refund when you don't have to. There's no better way to get glowing even gushing feedback comments. On more than one occasion, I have given a refund when shipping costs a flat $9.99 and postage costs, say, only $5.

557. Ship as quick as you can. It's common to finish sales on a Sunday night. If someone pays instantly with PayPal, try to ship out Monday morning if you can. Your buyers are sure to be pleased if they receive an item just a day or two after the end of a sale.

558. It's confession time: once I mixed up two pairs of shoes because I was in hurry and couldn't remember what boxes they were in. From that time on, I printed out two copies of each shipping statement. One goes in the box. The other is taped to the outside of the box. It enables me to double check the address and to see quickly whether or not someone has paid for insurance. The second statement also serves as a record of when the item is shipped, when I add the date. Such a record comes in handy when a shipment is lost or delayed.

559. Be sure to get delivery confirmation when you ship domestically. Ninety-nine percent of the time, you won't need it. But if your buyer claims it didn't arrive when it actually did in an attempt to get a refund (it happens), you'll be able to track the package and verify to the buyer that it was actually delivered. Delivery confirmation is free if you print your postage online using My eBay and the U.S. Postal Service's Priority Mail, by the way.

560. If you print out your own postage, be sure your postage costs don't actually appear on the package. Your buyers will quickly be able to calculate the difference between what you charged them for shipping and the actual postage cost. If the difference is more than a dollar or two, you might get a complaint and a request for a refund.

561. You don't have to use the U.S. Postal Service if you want to print out your own postage. Endicia Internet Postage (http://www.endicia.com) enables you to print out many different kinds of postage online, including overseas postage, which can be difficult to handle on your own due to customs restrictions. Standard service at this writing costs $9.95 per month.

13.

Shipping Domestically and Internationally

Once you've done your packing and calculated postage, you have to get your merchandise out the door. Shipping from state to state can quickly become routine as long as you follow the suggestions presented in this chapter. Shipping to other countries is not so routine. Everything becomes more complicated when packages go overseas: you have to choose unusual shipping options, you have to fill out customs forms, you have to estimate higher charges. If you are able to overcome these hurdles, however, it's well worth the effort. You open your merchandise to a far wider audience than ever before. And some things that are in demand overseas just don't experience the same demand in your own country. All you need is a little planning and few helpful suggestions, such as the ones I present here.

562. It's time-consuming and difficult to pack fragile items and ship them long distances. Don't scrimp on shipping expensive and delicate collectibles. Double-box, use plenty of packing material, and take out insurance.

563. Some buyers will do anything to save a few bucks. One asked me to ship shoes Parcel Post instead of Priority Mail; one Japanese buyer wanted me to ship shoes in a big envelope to get the lower rate. Remember the customer is (usually) always right. Tell him you aren't responsible for any damage or delays that can occur if you use the cheapest possible shipping methods. Then give him what he wants. He'll be happy and reward you with good feedback for your flexibility.

564. If you have ever considered hiring someone to help you, even if it's only on a part-time basis, shipping is the task to consider. Because it's repetitious by nature, shipping can easily be broken into a series of steps that employees can easily understand.

565. As previously mentioned, high school students are perfect as assistant shippers because they can work for a couple of hours in the afternoon and help you get packages out the door. This leaves you to focus on other essentials like creating listings, photography, and bookkeeping.

566. Don't leave shipping to the last minute. Suppose your post office closes at 6:30 p.m. Don't start packing and labeling at 6 o'clock. Give yourself a couple of hours. I'm speaking from experience—when you're in a hurry and rushing to get to the car and then get to the post office on time, you can easily make mistakes such as mixing up packages or shipping out the wrong items.

SHIPPING DOMESTICALLY

567. If you can locate your warehouse or office near an airport or other postal hub, you'll be able to ship your merchandise out that much faster. You might gain a day or two over the competition and you'll be able to really impress your customers. Take this into account if you're looking for workspace.

568. When you're ready to ship, if you've already printed out your postage and affixed it to your package, save yourself a trip to the post office. You can schedule a pickup by your friendly neighborhood mail carrier. Go to www.usps.com, click Schedule a Pickup, and follow the instructions that appear on the next screens.

569. Make friends with your postal employees. Be sure to give out holiday gifts. You'll be seeing a lot of them and depending on them. Your shipping will go more smoothly if you can count on their cooperation.

570. As previously mentioned, ask your post office if you can deliver to the loading dock or the back door of the facility once you print out your own postage. You shouldn't have to wait in line if you've done the bulk of the work already.

571. Don't gouge your buyers by charging them too much for shipping and handling. They can turn to the USPS Postal Calculator (http://ircalc.usps.gov) just as you can. After they receive your package, they can weigh it and determine just how much you charged. A few will complain. A dollar or two is quite reasonable for all your time and effort. More than that, and you're beginning to gouge.

572. I usually charge a flat fee of $9.99 for shipping shoes. When I'm in a hurry, I forget to change the shipping charge when I'm sending out heavy hiking boots or work boots. When the postal shipping charge comes back as $11 or $12, I'm disappointed. Don't make the same mistake: change the shipping charge beforehand so you don't lose money.

SHIPPING OVERSEAS

573. Be sure you estimate a high enough charge for international shipping to cover your expenses. A two- or three-pound package sent to Europe Global Priority can easily cost $25. Don't lose money when you ship because you underestimated and included a flat rate for shipping in your auction description that turned out to be too low.

574. Global Priority packages have size limitations. They can't be bigger, or else you have to send the package Air Parcel Post. Before you say in your listing that you can send something Global Priority, make sure the item will fit in the box. Packages can't be more than four pounds, either. Check the USPS website (pe.usps.com/text/Imm/immc2_016.html) for more details.

575. Mark overseas packages as a "gift" on the customs form. I know, this isn't technically correct. But if you mark the item as a purchase or a sale, customs may very well charge your customers an extra fee. And they are getting a gift in a way, aren't they?

576. When you value your item on the customs form you are required to fill out for overseas customers, limit the value to the purchase price, not the total including shipping or insurance. You don't want them to pay any more in customs than they have to.

577. If you ship jewelry or gemstones overseas, check with your shipper first. You may have to fill out special forms or meet other special requirements.

578. There's a page on eBay's site that's devoted to the subject of international trading. Some of the tips cover shipping. You'll find it at pages.ebay.com/internationaltrading/internationalseller.html.

579. Canadian buyers are sometimes surprised at how much they are charged to receive what they purchase on eBay. Rather than getting a good deal because they're buying from their neighbor right across the border, they are hit with customs, duties, and taxes. If someone makes a purchase from you from Canada, it's a good idea to make him aware of these charges.

580. If you frequently sell to Canada, you may want to set up a Non-Resident Importer Account. You can then bill your customers up front for taxes and other charges along with your usual shipping charges. It's more work for you, but it will make life easier for your customers and may attract more purchases from Canada.

581. Most shipping companies will automatically insure shipments to other countries for $100. If your item is worth more than this, you may want to remind your buyers that insurance will be extra.

582. If you sell to Canada and you use UPS, make sure insurance is available. UPS doesn't insure some household items like computers, clothing, and electronics.

583. On the other hand, UPS has its good points if you sell overseas. If you use UPS Worldwide Express or other extra-fast services, they include automatic customs clearances.

584. For items with a value higher than $2,500, you may need a special form called a Shipper's Export Declaration. Check with your shipper for more details.

585. If you ship to Mexico or Canada, your items might be subject to the NAFTA treaty agreements. These destinations require a Certificate of Origin.

586. Items like alcoholic beverages, plants, seeds, tobacco, and any perishable commodities are prohibited by many countries outside the United States (as well as within the U.S.). UPS provides a list of Restricted and Prohibited Items at www.ups.com/content/us/en/resources/select/sending/customs/prohibited.html.

587. Shippers like UPS also restrict some items that eBay doesn't normally restrict, such as artwork, precious metals, and magnets. See the web page listed in the preceding tip for more information.

588. Keep in mind that international shipments are going to undergo much more handling than those done domestically.

SHIPPING BULKY AND OVERSIZE ITEMS

589. If you have really big and heavy items to sell, more work is involved. First and foremost, do some extensive research on eBay's current and completed sales. See if there is really a market for what you have.

590. If it seems like eBay is a waste of time and effort with regard to your over-size item, don't give up completely. Consider selling on your local version of Craigslist (http://www.craigslist.org).

591. You can either post photos on Craigslist, or you can include links to photos you've posted on your website. Take photos of your item from several angles and make them available online—or offer to email them to any interested parties.

592. Suppose there is a market on eBay for that big, bulky item. How do you sell it? The option followed by many sellers is to specify in the auction description that shipping will not be offered. Instead, you can specify that the item must be picked up by the purchaser.

593. Another option: get a shipping quote from Freightquote.com (http://www.freightquote.com). You'll have to weigh the item. And you'll have to sign up for the service. But Freightquote.com will arrange to pick up the item. And you get to add a calculator to your description so customers can determine the exact cost. It dramatically widens the range of possible buyers and makes it more likely that your item will sell.

594. If you have a bulky appliance to sell on eBay, your first consideration should be how you are going to pack and ship the object. If you have no way to weigh or package it, consider specifying "pickup only," in which the buyer is required to pick the item up or hire a shipper to do so.

595. If you have a heavy, bulky item and you want to maximize profits by selling it at auction, you need to measure its height, width, and depth. Write these down; you'll need to pass them on to the shipper at some point.

596. Weighing your piece of furniture is important. Suppose you guess the weight and guess too low. The buyer will be required to pay the shipping fee for that weight and no more. The shipper will invoice you for the additional cost.

597. If anything, overestimate the weight of your item. Your shipper will credit you for the balance and possibly give you a refund, if you ask for it.

598. Before you start guessing the weight of that dryer, range, or other appliance, look in the instruction manual. Or check the manufacturer's website. Or call the manufacturer and ask.

599. If all other avenues fail, how *do* you weigh the big heavy object? Get a big piece of plywood, and a floor scale that can accommodate at least as much as you think the object might weigh. Put the wood on the scale. Get some strong people to lift the item onto the wood. (You might need another person to steady the piece of wood.) Tell your "porters" to let go of the object, however briefly, while you record the weight.

600. When you weigh the object, don't forget other packing materials. If you need to mount the object on a pallet (a piece of wood that goes under freight), weigh that, too. Also include the weight of tape or other wrapping material.

601. Some shippers, like Freightquote.com, require you to purchase a pallet. You can buy these cheaply at a home supply store.

602. You may also need to shrink-wrap an item; go to the store and buy several boxes of sticky clear plastic, such as Saran Wrap. Wrap it around and around the object until it's protected completely from damage.

603. If you sign up for a free account with Freightquote.com, you get to add Freightquote's handy shipping calculator to your eBay auction descriptions. You enter the size and weight and zip code where the item is located. Prospective buyers can then add their own zip code to see how much shipping would cost.

604. Another shipper, uShip (www.uship.com), lets you specify whether you'll pack the item yourself (which is less expensive) or have the shipper do everything for you.

605. When photographing furnishings or appliances that you have stored in your basement or garage, be sure to cover any ugly walls with a clean white sheet. It makes your item look more desirable—or, if you prefer, less grungy.

14.

Returns and Other Problems

A survey conducted by eBay in July 2005 found that 21 percent of people who didn't buy something cited the lack of a return policy as the reason they decided to make a purchase somewhere else. Buyers feel they need a safety net. When you tell buyers that you will accept returns, you give them the measure of security they need. The trick is to strike a balance between giving buyers a measure of security and protecting your business investment as well.

606. Create a customer-friendly return policy. A policy that is clear and yet leaves customers feeling they can trust you is tricky to assemble, but it will protect you from disputes while encouraging purchases.

607. If you use eBay's Sell Your Item form, you don't have to do anything about creating a return policy if you don't want to. By default, the Returns Accepted box is checked, so eBay assumes you will take returns. You should take a minute or two to look at your options for accepting returns so you can customize your policy if you want to.

608. The Sell Your Item form isn't the only option you have for creating a return policy. You also get a space for adding a return policy in Turbo Lister. In fact, the options are the same in Turbo Lister. Plus, you can restate your return policy in the body of the description for extra emphasis.

A DOZEN ESSENTIAL ELEMENTS OF A RETURN POLICY

609. By default, the Sell Your Item form gives buyers seven days to return the item. Does that mean seven days from the time when you mailed it or seven days from when it was received? And do they really need a week to decide if they want it or not? You are well within your rights to change this to three days by choosing this option from the drop-down list in the Return Policy section of the Sell Your Item form.

610. The time provided for returns in the drop-down list in the Return Policy section includes several options of up to thirty days. I'm not sure why you would ever want to give a buyer an entire month to decide to return an item. In that month, the item might well be used, worn, and damaged by the buyer. I suggest you stick with the three- or seven-day option instead.

611. Another default option calls for you to give the buyer her money back. This certainly makes the buyer happy. But is it fair to you? Consider the other options—exchanging the unwanted item for another, or providing credit toward another purchase—which will help you move your inventory.

612. The Return Policy section of the Sell Your Item form gives you a whopping 302 characters in which to spell out a return policy in detail. You've got plenty of room for friendly warnings to customers, such as, "I know you'll be happy with what you purchase. But if you find that its condition or color don't match the description, I will readily refund your entire purchase cost or provide credit toward another purchase." These extra words aren't really necessary, but they give the buyer that much-needed safety cushion that will make it easier to follow through with a bid or purchase.

613. If you feel secure about your ability to sell your merchandise and resell items if they are returned, you might choose to adopt a "100 percent customer satisfaction" return policy. In your Terms of Sale, you would state something like, "Your satisfaction is guaranteed. If you are dissatisfied for any reason, you can receive a refund for the full purchase price." Usually, experienced PowerSellers are the ones who give such liberal return policies, but you are likely to get more bids if you say this because you develop a higher level of trust.

614. It's important to say "refund for the full purchase price" in your return statement. Otherwise, you'll end up paying for several shipping charges. If the customer is returning the item only because he doesn't like it, and not because it is damaged or does not match your description, you shouldn't have to pay for shipping. On the other hand, if you made a mistake, you should offer to pay for shipping. You'll take a big loss, but you were the one who made the mistake.

615. A less liberal return policy would state that you will accept returns if the item is damaged in transit, if it is the wrong item, or if the item does not match your description. If the customer simply changes her mind, you don't have to accept her return.

616. Be clear about what you won't accept from customers in terms of money or complaints. In your auction descriptions, include a stock boilerplate paragraph that describes the types of payments you won't accept, or the reasons why you won't accept returns.

617. Many big-time traditional retailers charge a restocking fee of customers who return merchandise. You can do this too, particularly if a return means that one of your employees has to spend time unpacking, restocking, and marking the item back in inventory. That's time lost, and time is money, so it's not out of line for you to charge a dollar or two for this service. Don't gouge buyers by charging $5 or more, however.

618. Be clear about the condition of the item when it is returned to you. Tell the buyer that you will only accept the item in its original unopened box, if you sent it in the box. If they open the box or packaging and send it back to you, it's lost value and won't resell for as much as it did the first time. You also don't want fragile items rattling around in the box any more than your buyers want it. You might specify that the buyer send the item back with packing material.

619. It doesn't hurt to repeat your return policy in the body of your sales description. This builds even more trust in buyers. The second mention doesn't need to be lengthy. You might say, "Returns accepted (see Terms of Sale below)", and leave it at that. Or you can craft a more detailed description.

620. Some sellers include a blanket statement with their auction descriptions that states, in effect: "Your satisfaction is guaranteed." That means if the buyer is dissatisfied for any reason, they can return the item for any reason within a certain period (say, ten days). Don't leave it at that. Take advantage of the space available to you and be specific. The more specific you are, the less your chances of a dispute.

PROTECTING YOURSELF AGAINST LOSS AND TROUBLE

621. Taking lots of photos and being upfront about sizes, brand names, model numbers, or flaws in your auction descriptions will reduce the number of returns you'll be forced to make. It's always a good idea to point out any flaws openly; it not only prevents conflict, but it makes you look more trustworthy.

622. If you cheerfully give a full refund, you'll make your customer happy, but make sure you actually get your item returned. If the reason for the refund is that the buyer has changed his mind, refund only for the purchase price, not shipping costs. But if the reason is a mistake on your part (you shipped the wrong item, for instance), include shipping in the refund amount.

623. If you're suspicious about who might bid on your item or if you're selling something really important, pre-approve your bidders. This gives you the ability to assemble a list of people who indicate their interest and who are required to email you for approval before they are allowed to bid. Go to the Managing Bidders and Buyers page (http://pages.ebay.com/help/sell /manage_bidders_ov.html), click Pre-Approve a List of Bidders/Buyers for a Particular Listing, and fill out the form.

624. Don't throw away your photos. It's rare, but it happens: a buyer claims an item was damaged or arrived in worse condition than advertised. Having the original photos on hand helps you prove your description was accurate.

625. A tracking number (also called a delivery confirmation number) is essential. You get delivery confirmation for free when you ship online using Priority Mail. Otherwise, you have to pay a nominal fee (or pass all or part of the cost on through a handling fee) for delivery confirmation. The number helps you avoid disputes by letting you prove whether something was delivered or not.

626. If you're looking to avoid problems like the ones described in this chapter, be sure you know beforehand what eBay considers illegal. Be aware of the list of Prohibited Items (http://pages.ebay.com/help/policies/items-ov.html). You'll know what not to buy when you hit the flea markets and garage sales.

627. Suppose you have a dozen or more sales ending at 10 p.m. local time on a Saturday night. You should check those sales to make sure they're accurate. The time to check is first thing Saturday morning by 10 a.m., if not sooner. If a sale ends in less than twelve hours, you cannot add information to it or correct it. If a sale ends in more than twelve hours, you can make corrections if no bids have been placed. If bids have been placed, you can at least add information.

628. It would be only logical, you might argue, to have a friend or relative place bids to hike up the price of an item you're selling. Even after you divide your ill-gotten gain, you are still ahead of the game, you might protest. That is a very bad method called bid collaboration or shill bidding. Just say no.

629. Another temptation might be not to involve anyone else, but to use a secondary User ID on your own to artificially raise the level of bidding or the price on your own item. If eBay finds out that you've done such a thing, you could well be thrown out of eBay on your eEar.

DEALING WITH PROBLEMS

630. It's rare, but it does happen occasionally: sometimes you receive threats from people who feel they have been mistreated by you in some way. If you receive actual threats of physical violence, you can contact your local law enforcement officials. You should also contact the Internet service provider of the person sending the threat—it's almost certainly a violation of their rules of usage.

631. Being a successful seller is a dream come true, but it could turn into a nightmare if you are knowingly or unknowingly involved in dishonest practices. If someone approaches you with a scheme in mind that sounds too good to be true, it probably is. Run, don't walk, in the opposite direction.

632. In another naughty ploy (kind of like *The Producers*, where they tried to make a bad play on purpose), two people in cahoots with the seller try to lose the auction. It's called bid shielding when one person bids a very low amount and the other bids a very high amount. At the last minute, the high bid is pulled away (after also having served the purpose of discouraging other bidders), and the low bid wins. Again, the User ID is probably a phony because this activity is cause for suspension. If you see this happen with one of your sales, report it to eBay right away.

633. Something else that gives sellers a bad name is called bid siphoning. It involves emailing bidders in an auction to ask them to bid on or buy something else, or trying to steer them to something similar for a bargain price. The bad guy will commonly urge his prey to complete the deal off eBay. All this is definitely not the way to go.

634. Hijacking doesn't occur only on the high seas. There are those who use hijacked eBay accounts to defraud others of their money. Secondary User IDs are also common ways to work mayhem. Go ahead and be a tattletale. The more experienced you become as a seller the more sensitive your nose can get in sniffing out trouble. The way to fight them is to blow the whistle. You might not be able to save the auctions that they mess up, but you can learn to recognize such problems and avoid them in the future.

635. If you do encounter a dispute with a buyer, turn to eBay's Resolving Disputes page (pages.ebay.com/help/tp/problems-dispute-resolution.html). It's got the basics on how to deal with problems that come up occasionally in the marketplace. Remember that you're hardly the first seller to run into trouble, and there are well-established procedures for resolving disagreements peacefully.

636. Suppose a buyer complains that the item purchased is not as you described it: the color is wrong, the number of flaws is different, the size is not what you said it was. You have a choice. Many sellers will simply take the item back and resell it. If you find that the buyer is disagreeable about the complaint and the complaint itself is unfounded, you can open up a special case with eBay called an Item Not Received or Significantly Not as Described process.

637. The process referred to in the preceding tip is a lengthy one. You should get an idea of the steps involved by going to pages.ebay.com/help/tp/inr-snad-process.html and reading about it.

638. The key word in the preceding tips is "significantly." Unfortunately, this one word gives the buyer leeway to make a complaint. The buyer might claim that a flaw he discovered is significant. But you might think it's insignificant. As a result, you have a dispute. This is another reason to make your descriptions as accurate as you can and take as many photos as you can that show any cracks or other flaws clearly.

639. If the buyer paid for the item that's in dispute using PayPal, don't use the eBay dispute process mentioned above. You have to turn to PayPal's own claims system to resolve the dispute.

640. One of the hardest situations you can run into is the member who refuses to pay for something and then abandons eBay altogether or moves on to a new User ID to avoid an Unpaid Item strike and negative feedback. There's not much you can do about such a person except to file the Unpaid Item dispute. You can then either resell the item or make a Second Chance Offer to an underbidder, if there was one.

641. You start the dispute process, like many other processes, from My eBay. On the left side of the page under the heading My eBay Views, click Dispute Console. Then select the type of dispute you want to open.

642. You'll need your item number; scroll across it to highlight it and press Ctrl+C to copy it to your clipboard. When you open a dispute, you can click in the appropriate box and press Ctrl+V to paste it in. That way you don't have to write it down by hand—or try to remember it.

643. Suppose someone complains that she is unhappy with your item. Rather than simply giving in and providing a refund, or opening a dispute file, there's a third alternative. You can offer another item you have in stock for free.

644. Keep the big picture in mind when you encounter an unhappy customer. In most cases, simply giving in, giving the customer what he wants, and moving on to more profitable activities will serve you better than getting bogged down in arguments.

645. Turn to a third party when possible to help resolve your dispute. Try to get eBay's Investigations team involved. Some warning flags follow eBay users, and if you see someone with one of the flags next to her User ID, you should be aware of it. A zero (0) feedback rating isn't necessarily a problem—everybody has to start somewhere, after all. But negative feedback is discouraged by many sellers. Another person who will put you in a dilemma is a NARU. This individual is Not a Registered User, usually because of being suspended by eBay, and isn't supposed to buy or sell. If, however, they somehow manage to place a bid and win, you're not obligated to go through with the sale. But you might be tempted to do so anyhow.

15.

Communicating with Customers and Other eBay Members

One reason for eBay's success is the emphasis placed on responsiveness and general good behavior on the part of all members. Email is the primary medium for showing prospective customers that you care about them and are committed to ensuring that they have a good experience buying from you. It's all about training yourself to develop a good attitude. If you're used to getting angry at drivers who cut you off in traffic or at unsolicited phone calls from telemarketers, you've got to learn some new habits. You've got to develop a thick skin and take a deep breath before responding to negative comments. You've got to stick to the high road and be courteous and responsive at all times. Some easy-to-follow tips and tricks for keeping your communication productive are explored in this chapter.

646. If you simply can't agree with someone or stop an unpleasant series of interactions, turn to a mediator for help. SquareTrade (www.squaretrade.com) offers a dispute resolution service for eBay sellers when all else fails.

647. If someone leaves you feedback that you find unreasonable, don't let it stand. Add a clarification using the Respond to Feedback feature.

648. When you're working out your budget, be sure to allow for the inevitable NPB. That stands for nonpaying bidder—someone who wins an auction and fails to respond, or who does respond but never follows through on a transaction by sending payment. Hopefully that won't happen too often, but it's better to prepare for it.

649. You can provide insurance for your buyers and gain the ability to display a "seal of approval" logo on your auction listings if you qualify to become a Bonded Seller with BuySAFE (http://www.buysafe.com). You have to apply to the program, and you have to pay 1 percent of the final sale price of any item you sell through the program. But BuySAFE contends that you get more bids, and higher bids, because of the higher level of trust you communicate to other members.

GENERAL EMAIL TIPS

650. Email is the primary communication method for eBay members. To keep relations positive, learn the basics of netiquette, the set of rules and behaviors that govern email and other communications. When you don't see other correspondents face-to-face, you have to find ways to avoid misunderstanding and create a good mood. For instance, use greetings like "Hi," and sign-off phrases like "Best wishes" or "Sincerely."

651. Here's a simple rule that applies to all communications on eBay and most email messages: don't respond right away. Think about what you want to say first. Give yourself at least five or ten minutes to compose a professional and positive response.

652. Emoticons, also called smileys, originated long before the Web. They can go a long way toward portraying emotions via email. You can often soften a harsh message or bad news if you use one. Scan the list at http://www.emoticon.com.

653. A TLA is a *three-letter acronym*. If someone uses one in an email message to you, use one in kind. BTW (by the way) and LOL (laughing out loud) are popular TLAs seen frequently on eBay.

654. If you are having an argument that you can't seem to get out of, just let it go. Tell the other party you're not going to prolong the discussion any further, and simply stop.

SECURITY ISSUES

655. You may think you have chosen the perfect password, but don't be too hasty in congratulating yourself. Make sure nobody is looking over your shoulder to see what keys are being pressed. Don't write it down on a sticky note attached to your computer, in your notebooks, or on a piece of paper, no matter how far you shove it into a drawer.

656. Don't be hard on yourself if you run into trouble and lose your 100 percent positive feedback rating. Even the best PowerSellers get a few negative feedback comments once in a while. As long as you keep these to a minimum, you should be able to keep your feedback rating above 95 percent, which is still a very respectable figure.

657. eBay is a do-it-yourself kind of place, all right, but that doesn't mean you have to take care of all problems by yourself. The Security & Resolution Center (http://pages.ebay.com/securitycenter/) is the place to turn if you run into a buyer who won't pay for an item he purchased, or if you encounter another problem with a transaction.

658. Identity theft is a very real problem with regard to eBay. Hackers and criminals will do anything to get their hands on your credit card information or your User ID and password. Avoid responding to any email messages you receive telling you your security has been compromised, or asking you to verify your account information. eBay will never send you an email message asking for such information.

659. Your customers are just as concerned about trust as you are. They want to know with certainty that you are who you say you are and that you aren't a hacker pretending to sell something so you can collect the money without delivering. You can put their minds at ease by applying to eBay's ID Verify program. You have to pay a $5 fee for this service. In return, you get a special ID Verify icon you can display along with your User ID. Find out more at http://pages.ebay.com/services/buyandsell/idverify-login.html.

660. "Spoof" sites—sites that pretend to be eBay and that attempt to get you to submit your personal and financial information fraudulently—are among the biggest security risks on eBay. The eBay Toolbar has a feature called Account Guard that warns you when you are viewing a site that is potentially fraudulent. Download the toolbar and try it out.

GENERAL COMMUNICATION ISSUES

661. Come up with a stock response to members who point out a typo or discrepancy in your description. For instance: "Thank you for pointing out the error. I am correcting this and the new information should be online by the time you read this."

662. Don't be impatient with people who point out that you've done something wrong. No matter what their motivation is, it doesn't matter. They've helped you to prevent further confusion that will keep you from getting bids and wasting insertion fees. Swallow your pride, fix the mistake, and move on. Whatever you do, don't respond negatively.

663. Buyers don't realize that you need to wait until they have received what you have shipped and are satisfied with it before you leave feedback for them. Don't be impatient when they ask you to leave feedback, even if they ask something like, "Don't you ever leave feedback for anyone?" Be patient and respond positively that you will do so as soon as your schedule permits.

664. Don't be coerced into giving feedback if you're not ready to do so. The feedback system only works if it's voluntary and people are truly being honest. Even if someone nags you about feedback, do it when it's convenient and doesn't interfere with your other sales activities.

665. You might occasionally get a question that's already covered in your description. Don't be snide or rude about your response. It's possible someone is sending you the question not because they want the answer but because they need to know whether or not you are a responsible and responsive seller. (I used to do this myself before placing a bid.)

666. Here's a stock response to the all-too-obvious question: "Thank you for your interest and for your question. As stated in the description, [fill in the blank with the answer]. Please don't hesitate to ask for more information, and happy bidding!"

667. It's always a good idea to save your stock email responses in the form of templates. That way you can use them over and over again. Compose them when you're in an even temper and not in the heat of battle. That way you can insert them as a reply and keep your emotions out of the picture.

668. Why, you may ask, is it so important to bend over backward to be nice to customers, even when they are being offensive? It's business—it's not personal. For decades, ever since Marshall Field uttered the phrase "Give the lady what she wants," sellers have emphasized customer service. You need to develop a professional reputation, and being positive at *all* times will help you do it.

669. As I noted in the previous chapter, a few customers make it their business to police how much they are charged for shipping and handling. You might end up earning $3-$5 through shipping if you charge a flat rate—it can happen through no fault of your own, if the destination is nearby and the package is light. If someone complains, give them a refund—but keep $1 for your handling charges. You deserve it!

DEALING WITH NON-RESPONSIVE BUYERS OR SELLERS

670. What happens if another member fails to respond to your messages, whether you send them via email or through eBay's message system? First of all, don't panic, and don't immediately assume the worst. There are several reasons why communication might not be working. The other person may be sick or out of town, or he may have a spam filter that is preventing your email messages from getting through.

671. If someone doesn't respond to you for more than a week, send her an invoice. I don't usually send invoices unless I need to remind someone to pay up. Buyers get invoices when they make a purchase and don't need another one from me. Don't accuse her of anything—don't say anything at all—just send the invoice.

672. If someone doesn't respond to your invoice reminder for three or four days, send another invoice. This time, add a stock message: "I have sent two invoices and haven't heard from you yet. If I don't hear from you in x days, I'll give you a phone call. After that I'll have to file an unpaid item case."

673. If you fail to hear from the member after your second reminder notice, click Advanced Search, and click Find Contact Information in the links on the left-hand side of the Search: Find Items page. Enter the member's User ID and the item number of the item you are trading with the person, and click Search. eBay will send an email message to both parties, with a street address and phone number. Often, this email alone will "flush" a nonresponsive bidder out, because it lets him know that eBay is taking an interest in him, not just you.

674. If a nonpaying bidder fails to get in touch with you within seven days after you file the Unpaid Item dispute, you can close the dispute. Doing so allows you to get back your Final Value Fee from eBay.

675. Here's another option if you can't contact a member immediately. If she has an About Me icon next to her User ID, click it. Take a look at the About Me page—you might find alternate contact information on it.

676. Keep a record of the nonpaying bidders. You don't want one of them to turn up in your sales months or years later and do the same thing to you again. You can ban such members from bidding on your sales. Go to http://cgi1.ebay.com/ws/eBayISAPI.dll? bidderblocklogin and login to initiate the process.

677. A record of nonpaying bidders will also ensure that you won't forget about needing to file an Unpaid Item form against someone. The list will also help you close the dispute so you can get a refund of your Final Value Fee.

678. If you only use the default email preferences eBay assigns you, your email inbox will be flooded with a stream of messages when you start selling: "You have been outbid," "Your bid has been received," and so on. If you want to cut down on such messages, change your preferences: go to My eBay, sign in, go to My Account, click eBay Preferences and then click the View/Change link next to Notification Preferences.

679. Are you tired of logging in continually? eBay does make you log in frequently—but this is a preference you can change. In the login page, check the box that lets you remain logged in as long as you are on the site.

16.

Increasing Your Productivity

What separates a regular seller from a PowerSeller? Some people would say the answer is time—PowerSellers must have more time to devote to their business. Others would say experience—they must simply be better sellers than most others. I say no to both assertions. The difference is actually productivity. PowerSellers, who usually start out with little or no business experience and who are just as busy as the rest of us, find a way to list more items and ship out more merchandise than the rest of us.

680. Consider signing up for an account with a well-known auction service provider such as Vendio, Zoovy, or Channel Advisor. Such services cost a monthly fee, but they can pay off in the long run because of the time they save. At the very least, they can streamline tedious and repetitive practices such as relisting items or responding to feedback.

681. Come up with a system for conducting sales. Focusing on the same type of item and selling it over and over can help you complete more transactions in a given period of time.

682. Selling sets of items that vary slightly in size, color, or other attributes makes it relatively easy to turn around dozens or even hundreds of sales descriptions. You create a single listing template and use it over and over, making small changes as needed.

683. eBay is one of the most effective marketplaces for acquiring customers. To keep those customers coming back for repeat purchases, do some cross-promotion: when someone is shopping for one item, suggest others they might be interested in as well. Many auction providers, such as Vendio, make this easy for you. You can also do cross-promotion in My eBay; click Cross Promotion Connections under My Account, and set up this tool, which displays a See More Great Items box in each of your auction listings.

684. If you use a wholesaler or drop-shipper as your supplier, ask for stock photos. You can insert their photos instead of taking your own fresh photos over and over again, which will free up lots of time for you to create more sales descriptions.

685. How do some sellers manage to put up hundreds of items in their stores at a time? They don't always have dozens of employees. Rather, they create a single template for a type of item, such as a suit or a golf ball. Then, they sell many different variations on that item. For instance, they take a photo of a blue suit. Then they offer many different sizes of the suit. For their one listing, they might be able to create a dozen or more separate sales descriptions. Think about selling merchandise that comes in many different sizes and model numbers.

686. If something doesn't sell the first time, relist it. Two times—relist it again. It often takes two or three listings to sell something. Don't give up on it right away. This seemingly simple concept is sure to boost your sales rate.

687. After an item fails to sell for a third time, put it up for sale in your eBay Store. If you let it sit on your shelves, you don't stand any chance of making money—and the description will disappear from My eBay after sixty days.

688. Even if one of your sold or unsold items is removed from your My eBay page because more than sixty days have passed, you may still be able to retrieve it. Click Advanced Search near the top of any eBay page. Click Completed Items, and enter as much of the title as you can remember. You just might be able to find your sale in the search results, even if more than sixty days have passed—it's worked for me.

689. Even if your item doesn't get bids, don't throw it away. I am continually surprised by email messages from people who suddenly remember a pair of shoes I had for sale at one time that is no longer for sale on eBay. As I was writing this book, I just got an inquiry for a pair of shoes I had forgotten about—but I still had them in my basement storage area. I dusted them off, put them for sale in my eBay Store, and made $13.

ANALYZING YOUR SALES

690. If you are plagued by lots of unsold items, you need to get systematic and do some analysis. Calculating your sell-through rate (STR) is critical for all sellers. STR is the ratio of items offered for sale in a given period divided by the number of those items that actually sold. If you offered ten items on Sunday and four of them sold, your STR is 40 percent.

691. It's also important to calculate the average sale price (ASP) of the items that sold. Add up the sale price of all the items that sold in a particular period—a day, a month, a year, and so on. Don't worry about Final Value Fees or Insertion Fees. You're only concerned with the gross sale price. Divide the total by the number sold. If you sold five pairs of gloves for $15, $12, $9, $9, and $8, your total is $53, and your ASP is $10.60.

692. Once you have calculated your STR and ASP, ask yourself some questions. Are some items just impossible to sell? Could you sell more if you included more photos or highlighted your sales?

693. Make note of the brand names, colors, and types of items that have the highest STR. Focus on building your inventory of those items, and don't purchase the ones with low STRs.

694. Pay attention to the STR not only for individual items but for the *category* in which you sell most frequently. It can be tedious to analyze an entire category if you don't have special software that does the work for you, but you can do a rough approximation. Count the number of sales in a page full of completed transactions in a category. Then count how many of the sales prices are presented in green—these are the ones that sold. The red ones are unsold items. Do several pages worth of results, and calculate the ratio of sales to the number of completed transactions. The result is the sell-through rate.

695. If the STR for your category is low—say, 30 percent or less—you may want to rethink selling in that category altogether. It may just not be a popular area on eBay. There isn't any formula for what constitutes a strong sell-through rate. I'm reluctant to assign a firm number. A good STR is one you can achieve with some consistency most of the year. You might do better around November and December, and worse in January and February. In my own case, if I sell 50 percent of what I offer at auction in a given week, I am satisfied; anything higher than that is gravy.

696. Look at other subcategories related to yours and see if the STR is any better than the one you sell in. If you find a better one, you may want to make a switch.

697. Calculate the STR every two or three weeks for several months. Make a note to yourself to track the STR once in a while so you don't forget. That way, you can track the sales trend over time for that part of eBay.

698. If the STR for your category is going up over time, that's good. Stay where you are—you're in a category that is popular. Calculate your STRs for half a dozen or so items you have sold in that category to compare your STR to the STR for the entire category.

699. Suppose your STR is 40 percent while the STR of the entire category is 60 percent. You should take a look at what you're selling. There's no reason why you shouldn't be getting a 60 percent sell-through rate. After all, your competitors are.

700. Suppose your category STR is 30 percent while your personal STR is 60 percent. That's still cause for concern. Even though you have popular items, you're in a category that's considered a slow one. Your personal sales are likely to start dwindling over time. You should probably start looking for greener pastures before you are in trouble.

701. How am I doing? That's a question you never stop asking when you're in business for yourself. PayPal can provide some answers with its post-sale manager. If you already have a PayPal account, you can get free software to help you keep track of shipments, feedback, and payments. Log in to PayPal, click My Account, and then review the various pages that report on your recent sales: Overview, Add Funds, History, Resolution Center, and Profile.

702. This might seem unlikely if you're just starting out, but many PowerSellers boosted their productivity by developing their own software solutions. In most cases, they worked with software developers to create applications that streamlined processes like feedback and relisting.

703. You'll find plenty of ideas for boosting sales in eBay's own newsletter, the Chatter (pages.ebay.com/community/chatter/). You'll find profiles of real-world sellers on eBay who explain how they achieved success or boosted profits on the marketplace.

704. If you only sell sporadically and you want to turn your sales hobby into a full-time job, find new wholesale suppliers. Review the tips in chapters 2 and 3 to expand your sources of merchandise.

CHOOSING THE RIGHT SALES SOFTWARE

705. The easiest option for listing multiple sales and designing auction descriptions easily is eBay's own Turbo Lister. The program is free to use. There is a cost, though, in terms of disk space; you need to download and install the software on your computer.

706. It's getting more and more difficult to find eBay's own sales management software on its site. I'm not sure why. But you'll find a handy comparison table listing the features of Turbo Lister, Selling Manager, and Blackthorne Basic and Pro at pages.ebay.com/selling_manager /comparison.html.

707. Turbo Lister is the software I use personally. It's big, bulky, and a memory hog, and it sometimes runs very slowly. But it gets the job done and does everything I need right now. The best thing about Turbo Lister: it makes it easy to set up sales templates and apply them.

708. Turbo Lister also lets me schedule listings so they can all begin at the same time. Once I prepare the sales, I can either start them all at once or schedule them to start in the future.

709. Turbo Lister needs to be updated periodically in order to keep up with eBay's new description features, but you are given the option to update the software automatically after you are finished uploading sales descriptions.

710. My eBay: this resource appeals to everyone who loves something for free—which is just about everyone on eBay. It's convenient—you don't have to do anything to set it up; just click the My eBay button in the toolbar to access it. My eBay is so convenient, in fact, that you can easily forget that other software is available to help you track and manage sales. The most obvious productivity tools are the ones offered by eBay itself—Turbo Lister, Selling Manager, and Blackthorne Basic and Pro. Since the software choices all have free trial options, it's worth your while to try them out.

711. Selling Manager is a sales management tool, as the name implies, and not a tool for creating listings. In fact, Selling Manager makes a good complement to Turbo Lister. It helps you track sales that are ongoing; it's a souped-up version of the My eBay Items I'm Selling View.

712. Selling Manager is particularly good post-sale. It lets you print invoices, for instance, and gives you templates for email communications. You get a monthly summary of all the sales you've archived—archiving sales is one of the great limitations of My eBay.

713. Selling Manager Pro is software you access with your browser rather than download to your computer. It lets you create sales and manage post-sale activities. It costs $15.99 per month; find out more at pages.ebay.com/selling%5Fmanager%5Fpro/.

714. Blackthorne Basic (formerly known as Seller's Assistant Basic) is a souped-up alternative to Turbo Lister. It too is software you download and install on your computer, and it requires 50MB of hard disk space. But it's not free; it carries a $9.99 monthly fee. Find out more at pages.ebay.com/blackthorne/basic.html.

715. Blackthorne Basic has sales management features that Turbo Lister doesn't have. It lets you manage email messages by applying templates. And it lets you track your current sales like My eBay.

716. Blackthorne Pro (formerly known as Seller's Assistant Pro) is also desktop software. But it has advanced business features that are designed for companies with multiple employees. This tool, which costs $24.99 per month and needs to be installed on each desktop that will use it, provides different views for each employee.

717. Blackthorne Pro has supply chain management features that the other programs don't have. It lets you track consignments and keep in touch with your suppliers. Find out more at pages.ebay.com/blackthorne/pro.html.

THIRD-PARTY SOFTWARE OPTIONS

718. Third-party vendors give you everything you need in one package. If you need help automating feedback and email responses because you're overworked, or if you need photo storage space as well as email service, turn to one of the auction service providers listed in Appendix A. SpareDollar (www.sparedollar.com) is especially inexpensive, but Vendio, Zoovy, and ChannelAdvisor are also very popular, especially among PowerSellers.

719. A tool like Andale Research helps you gather lots of market data for your category. Make sure the solution you sign up for includes Traffic Reports. These reports can tell you where your traffic is coming from so you can see which resources are most popular. Consider advertising with those sources.

720. Traffic reports can also tell you how many people are *converted* by each of the websites or individuals who refer customers to your eBay Store or your auctions. A shopper is converted when he takes an action. In the case of eBay, conversions consist of bids, purchases, or new memberships.

721. To be on the cutting edge, you should look for software that monitors not only eBay but other marketplaces like Over stock.com and Amazon.com. You should branch out to sell additional merchandise in those venues to supplement your eBay sales.

722. Big players in the ASP field such as ChannelAdvisor (www.channeladvisor .com), Marketworks (www.marketworks.com), and Infopia (www.infopia.com) all cover multiple marketplaces. You may have to pay a little more each month to play with the big boys, but you'll be able to gather and analyze more data and branch out to more e-commerce sites.

723. When you're analyzing sales data on eBay, keep in mind that not all of the sales figures may be accurate. Sometimes bids are driven to artificial heights through a process described earlier known as shill bidding. Shill bidding occurs when two or more bidders agree to work together to drive bids up, forcing other members to pay inflated prices.

17.

eBay Stores

An eBay Store is one of the key elements that can turn your sales efforts into success. A store might seem like an extravagance if you look at it from the viewpoint of someone who only sells occasionally on eBay and wants to make a few bucks on the side every month. But if you want to generate consistent income from eBay and turn your on-the-side activities into a productive business, a store gives you a professional business presence. It supplements your auctions and gives you another way to reach the public. This chapter presents some useful principles to follow when establishing and managing your eBay Store.

724. You can't open an eBay Store right away. You have to be registered as an eBay seller, and either have a feedback rating of twenty or more, go through eBay's ID Verify system, or have a PayPal account in good standing. It's a good incentive to build up your feedback right away by making some purchases or by completing some auction transactions.

725. Many eBay sellers are turned off by the minimum $15.95 per month rental fee for an eBay Store. But you might only have to sell one or two items from your store inventory in order to make up that fee. Take advantage of the thirty-day free trial period and see if you can make the fee back. If not, you can cancel the store; if you pass the test, keep the store online and keep marketing it using strategies outlined in this chapter.

726. Personally, I don't suggest opening an eBay Store unless you meet one of the following criteria: you have lots of items to sell at fixed price, you plan to update your inventory regularly, or you already have a feedback rating of fifty or more. If you are a PowerSeller, so much the better; you need a foundation of feedback and trust to make your store successful.

727. What's the single best thing about having an eBay Store? After all, stores do cost at least $15.95 per month. The best thing is that the typical listing only costs 2 cents. Add a gallery photo, and you have a listing for only 3 cents.

728. It makes sense to start by opening up a Basic Store. If you achieve a good sales rate and want to grow your sales rate more aggressively, you can open a Featured Store. Only open an Anchor Store if you sell on eBay for a living and you can make back the $499.95 per month fee.

729. Take some time deciding on a name for your store. Your store's name reflects on your business and on you personally. Find a name that's short and easy to remember and that ties in with the kinds of items you typically sell.

730. When you open your store, make sure you have a good selection of things to sell. Your inventory should be broad as well as deep. Come up with as many custom categories as you can.

731. Make your categories specific. For instance, instead of simply having the categories "Men's Shoes" and "Women's Shoes," I break them into "Men's Shoes size 11–11.5," "Men's Shoes size 10–10.5," and so on. It makes you look more professional and builds confidence in your shoppers.

732. eBay Store sales have to include a fixed Buy It Now price. But if you want some flexibility or aren't sure whether or not your price is competitive, check the Best Offer box when you create the sale. You give your shoppers the chance to effectively suggest a sale price. You don't have to accept the offer if you think it's too low.

733. eBay Stores give you several options when it comes to the length of the sale. An item can remain online for thirty, sixty, or ninety days. You can even leave the item up for sale indefinitely by checking the Good Till Canceled option when you specify the length of the sale.

734. Conventional wisdom tells you not to list merchandise indefinitely, or your store inventory will seem stale. That's what I thought until someone made a purchase of a set of advertising art I had had online for three months. Take advantage of the Good till Canceled option instead of listing store items for thirty, sixty, or ninety days. Keep your store fresh by periodically adding new merchandise.

735. When you create your store, take advantage of Promotion Boxes. These are boxes you create that call attention to new items, closeouts, or special deals of one sort or another. Having just one promotion box makes you look more professional and on the ball as a seller.

736. You might not realize it at first, but an eBay Store includes photo hosting space. You get 1MB of photo space for free with the Basic Store, and more for the more expensive store options.

737. eBay is offering more and more free services, possibly in an effort to make up for the recent increase in eBay Store monthly fees. One of the best services available for free to all eBay Store owners is Selling Manager. Selling Manager lets you create customizable email templates, sales history, and automated feedback to multiple individuals.

738. If you sign up for Selling Manager for free (and I strongly suggest you do so), be sure to take advantage of bulk relisting. After a group of sales ends, you can relist the sales all at once rather than having to list each sale in turn, which you are forced to do in My eBay.

MARKETING YOUR STORE

739. eBay provides a variety of selling tools that can help you monitor and improve store performance. You can give customers the opportunity to subscribe to an email newsletter that tells them when you have changed inventory. You can (and should) make use of tools like Merchandising Manager to provide you with monthly reports on your sales data so you can improve your success rate.

740. A Basic Store subscription gives you the ability to send one hundred email messages through eBay's message system. This enables you to send a simple email newsletter to one hundred customers. Each additional email message costs only one cent.

741. Do your best to market your store by purchasing keywords and advertising the store on your business cards and messages you include with your shipped merchandise.

742. Make an effort to keep your store inventory fresh by adding new merchandise every week. Breaking your merchandise into multiple categories makes you look organized and makes your selection seem more extensive than it really is.

743. eBay Stores don't market themselves. Make links to your store wherever you can. The best link is one that appears in your auction description. (Add it in the Sell Your Item form in Turbo Lister.) Also link to your store from your About Me page and your personal web page.

744. Do everything you can to induce a buyer to go to your store from your website (or from another location outside of eBay). If you do, you'll receive a Store Referral Credit and get 75 percent of your Final Value Fee back from eBay for that sale.

745. One of the best ways to spread the word about your eBay Store is to create a simple promotional flyer. You can then include the flyer in the shipments you send out to those who win your auctions. eBay makes it easy to create your own store flyer. Find out more about it at pages.ebay.com/help/specialtysites/promotional-flyer-creating.html.

746. eBay Store listings appear in a section at the bottom of search results. You can ensure that other search engines find your current store inventory listings by creating an XML file that describes your store's current content. You can then upload the file to search sites that support this feature. You'll find more information at pages.ebay.com/help/sell/contextual/export-listings.html.

747. Another innovative way to publicize your store is to create a Custom Listing Frame. Such a frame is inserted into your conventional (non-store) auction and Fixed Price sales. It can contain your store logo, your store search box, a list of categories in your store, and other store-related items.

748. Turn to advertising to promote your store. One of the newest and most efficient forms of advertising occurs when you purchase keywords through the eBay Keywords program (ebay.admarketplace.net/ebay/servlet/ebay). You tell eBay you'll pay, say, 50 cents to display a tiny ad bearing your store's name. If you sell baseball hats, you might buy the words "baseball cap," for instance.

749. You can also purchase advertising keywords through Google's AdWords program (adwords.google.com/select). Google does index the contents of eBay Stores.

750. You can also list your eBay Store in one of the free web directories that the search services provide. For instance, Yahoo!'s category-based directory of websites is one of the first and best-known. Listing your store increases the chances that you'll appear in a category and that the description will appear just the way you want it. Google's directory is at www.google.com/dirhp. To add your site, go to dmoz.org/add.html.

751. What are the most popular keywords entered in eBay's search form? Go to keyword-index.ebay.com/keyword-index.html. You can view the most popular keywords for the past week. You can also reach this page by clicking See All Popular Keywords in the left-hand column in any set of search results on eBay.

CREATING STORE SALES DESCRIPTIONS

752. If you already have an item listed at a thirty-day auction period, you can change it. You have to end the sale first by going to My eBay, clicking on the Selling link, and choosing the End Item link next to the sale's title. You can then change it to the Good Till Canceled option.

753. Keep in mind that if you schedule something to be listed in your store for more than thirty days, eBay hits you with a surcharge. Thirty-day sales cost 5 cents each with no surcharge. Good Till Canceled sales are charged 2 cents every thirty days.

754. When you design your store, you can choose colors that accent your store's home page and individual sales descriptions. Choose colors that complement any other web pages you have created, such as your website.

755. When you're pricing your eBay Store items, keep in mind that there's a significant price break at $25. At $25 or less, eBay charges 8 percent of the sales fee. For $25.01 or more, the Final Value fee is 8 percent of the first $25, plus 5 percent of the closing value balance.

756. I've already mentioned that eBay Store listings are dirt cheap, starting at 2 cents each with Gallery photos only 1 cent more. Subtitles only cost 1 cent extra for a thirty-day sale, and 2 cents for a Good Till Canceled sale—if you can include them, they're worth the expense.

CATEGORIES AND ORGANIZATION

757. When you create a store listing, you can only list the item in a category you have already set up within your store. You can't choose any eBay category. Keep in mind that an eBay Store can include as many as three hundred categories.

758. You can always change the categories within your store. Go to Manage My Store and check the box next to any categories you want to move. Then select the Move Category button. Select the destination category (the category where you would like to move the subcategories), and click Move.

759. Make sure your eBay Store category arrangement makes sense. You can arrange your categories by type of item or by size. You can also put your categories in alphabetical order if you wish.

760. If you don't have many categories, or if you would rather focus on creating sales descriptions than organizing categories, you can display eBay's relevant categories and subcategories rather than ones you create and name yourself. Go to Manage My Store, look for Display Settings, and click Change. You can then choose either eBay Categories or Store Categories.

761. Here's another suggestion for organizing categories: consider putting them in descending order. That way the categories that have the highest number of items for sale will be at the top of your category list. Buyers will have the chance to see the hottest and most active categories first when you do this.

762. How many people are actually visiting your eBay Store, and what do they do once they get there? You can use a feature called Traffic Reports to find out. You access this through Manage My Store.

763. There's yet another service that goes along with eBay Stores and is easily overlooked. It's called Accounting Assistant, and it enables you to export data from your eBay transactions into the popular accounting program QuickBooks. Find out more at pages.ebay.com/accountingassistant/.

764. eBay Stores are popular and help you supplement your auction sales, but they're not the only game in town. If you sign up for a monthly account with an auction service provider like Vendio (http://www.vendio.com), you can set up your own store for lower monthly fees than eBay charges.

765. What makes a good eBay Store name? It should be short (one to three words, ideally) and easy to remember. It doesn't have to have anything to do with your products or yourself. One of the biggest PowerSellers on eBay, Kevin Harmon, has a store called Inflatable Madness. It's crazy, but it's easy to remember.

766. Don't assume you should only have one eBay Store. Some of the highest-volume eBay PowerSellers have two or more separate stores. One store is for one type of merchandise (comic books, for example), and the other is for something completely different (say, movie posters and memorabilia).

767. Another approach is to put your newest items in one store, and use the second store to sell off excess inventory at a lower price. In either case, having two or more storefronts makes the merchandise easier for customers to find, provided you have lots of inventory to sell.

MEASURING TRAFFIC TO YOUR EBAY STORE

768. If you operate an eBay Store, you have access to Traffic Reports. Go to My eBay, sign in, and click Manage My Store under the heading My Subscriptions. Under Reports, click Traffic Reports. Sign in, agree to Omniture Organization, and to the Omniture website. (Omniture manages eBay traffic reports.) You can then view the reports on the My Summary page.

769. When you view reports, pay particular attention to the places that referred your customers. These are the web pages and keywords that brought the customers to your descriptions.

770. If you operate a Featured or Anchor Store, you have access to richer traffic reports than are available to Basic Store owners. You can view path reports, which show how and from where shoppers first came to your store, and how they exited. If they left without purchasing, you might want to revamp the page they left from.

771. Bidding and Buying reports are also available to Featured and Anchor Stores. These indicate, among other things, the keywords and sites that referred your visitors. In other words, they show which of your marketing techniques are really working, so you can do more of the same.

Part Four:

Opening E-Commerce
Stores

PART FOUR

Opening E-Commerce Stores

18.

Weaving Your Own Website

Most of the successful eBay sellers I've interviewed over the years—the ones who have turned their sales efforts into full-time businesses—look at eBay as a very effective marketing tool, but not as an end in itself. eBay is unmatched as a way to introduce yourself to new customers. But once experienced sellers acquire those customers and build a level of trust, they try to steer those individuals to their websites so they can sell to them directly. It's not an either/or thing—you need eBay to get a foothold in the marketplace and establish your name. You also need a website to build a business identity and maximize profits by selling directly without having to pay fees to eBay or another marketplace. This chapter explores the elements of an effective e-commerce website and how to make your site complement your eBay sales presence.

772. At the very least, include the "must haves" for your website. These are your eBay User ID, your eBay Store address if you have one, your email address or other contact information, and links to your eBay sales.

773. Isn't an About Me page a small-scale website? It is. But you can have an About Me page and a website as well. Provide a link from your About Me page to a website where you sell to the public. Make the two sites work together to promote yourself and your sales.

774. A website isn't for everyone, but if you already work in a business that is related to your eBay sales categories, a site makes sense. You can promote your business in a way that supports both your online and offline sales.

775. Think about eBay as a great place to acquire customers. Once you have their contact information and their trust, what can you do? Steer them to your website, where you can sell to them via an online sales catalog.

776. When you sell through a web-based sales catalog, you have complete control over the presentation. You also get to collect all of the sales revenue, minus any sales tax you have to collect.

777. What's the first step in creating a website? Create a list of topics you want to discuss. Each web page on your site should discuss one (and only one) of those topics. Typical websites include a home page, a products page, an About Us page, a contact page, and individual item descriptions page.

778. Draw up a sketch of your site showing how the pages are linked to one another. The typical website structure takes the form of a pyramid. The home page is at the top. The second tier of pages presents the main categories of the site. The third tier consists of individual pages within each category.

779. You also need software that helps you create web pages. Some hosts provide you with the software as a rented service: you access some easy-to-use forms with your web browser and fill them out; when you submit the content to the site, your web pages are created.

780. If you want more control over the creation process, consider using an application that is specially designed to create web pages. Examples include Netscape Composer, Microsoft FrontPage, and Macromedia Dreamweaver.

WEB HOSTING SERVICES

781. You need to find a host for your website: an organization that is in the business of providing space on a web server to individuals or businesses like yours. Your ISP can function as a web host. Sites like AOL Hometown and Yahoo! GeoCities are well-known and affordable hosting services.

782. eBay itself operates a web hosting service called ProStores (http://www.prostores.com). Hosting packages start at $29.99 per month. This service is specially designed for e-commerce businesses; it includes a shopping cart and checkout system.

783. The obvious choice for hosting your website is your own ISP. Before you go through the effort of creating your web pages, make sure it's okay with your ISP to create a commercial website in the web server space that is allocated to you as part of your access account. Some ISPs prefer that you sign up for a web hosting account, which is intended especially for online businesses.

784. One of the advantages of signing up for a web hosting account, either with your ISP or another web host, is the ability to get two or more email addresses. You can allocate one address to business-related messages, one to eBay messages, one for personal use, and so on. That way any spam you receive can be insulated from your personal email account.

785. Yahoo! GeoCities (http://geocities.yahoo.com) has many advantages for first-time webmasters. GeoCities has been around for several years. It's now owned by Yahoo!, which is one of the best-known and most reputable online hosts. The site gives you a set of web forms that you fill out in order to design and upload your files so they appear online.

786. Tripod (http://www.tripod.lycos.com) has a free hosting option, but you have to display ads along with the web pages you create. If you don't mind that, you get 20MB of free web space, which is a little more than the 15MB that GeoCities provides. You also get the ability to create a blog, an online diary that can be for personal or business use—or both.

787. Earthlink (http://www.earthlink.com) is a popular service for Internet access. It also provides hosting services that include a web page creation tool called Click-n-Build.

788. If you're looking for an ISP or web host, you can't do much better than The List (http://thelist.internet.com). This site, which has been around for many years, organizes ISPs and web hosts by location and level of service so you can find what you're looking for quickly.

789. There's another place to look for a web host, and it's closer than you think. There are some eBay Stores that have been created to provide web hosting. Go to http://services.stores.ebay.com, click Web & Computer Services, and then click Web Hosting.

790. The Web & Computer Services area has some other resources that might come in handy when you are creating a website. Look for Technical Support and Web Hosting, for instance.

DOMAIN NAMES

791. At some point, you'll want to obtain a user-friendly domain name for your website. Make sure the host you choose lets you have one. A user-friendly domain name looks like this: http://www.gregholden.com. You have to choose a domain name that no one else has registered, which can be a challenge.

792. You also have to pay a registration fee to obtain the domain name you want and keep it for one year or more. Visit GoDaddy.com (http://www.godaddy.com) to search for a name and register it for a nominal fee.

793. Your website domain name will ideally fall into the dot-com category. In other words, it will have ".com" at the end of it. This is the most obvious domain name and the one that's easiest for prospective customers to remember.

794. If you can't find the name you want in dot-com, however, look for one of the many other domains, such as .us, .biz, or .net. The latter is intended for nonprofit institutions, but many eBay sellers use it for their websites (check out Blueberry Boutique, http://www.blueberryboutique.net).

795. What makes a good domain name? It needs to be short and easy to remember. That's all. It doesn't need to contain your personal name or even make sense. As previously mentioned, one of the biggest eBay sellers has the domain name Inflatablemadness.com, and he does just fine selling DVDs and CDs both on eBay and off.

796. When you do find a domain name you like, be sure to lock it down. In other words, pay the slightly higher fee to own it for at least three years, rather than one. Chances are you'll end up paying a lower fee per year than you would for a single-year contract.

797. If you can't locate a domain that's a single word, no problem. Try putting two words together. You can also separate them with hyphens like this: my-eBay-business.com. But if you can avoid hyphens, so much the better.

GOOGLE AND OTHER SEARCH ENGINES

798. Pay attention to the titles of the web pages you create. Titles are indexed by search engines. Make sure yours aren't blank. Include your store's name as well as one or two keywords describing what you sell. Make sure you include your store name and some important keywords into your web page headings. They too are indexed by search engine programs called robots or spiders.

799. The first fifty words of your home page should include as many keywords as you can gracefully cram into it. This text is indexed by the spiders, too.

800. Also make a commitment to keep your website updated on a regular basis. Even if you only add a sentence or two to a single page each day, it will help you. Search engines like Google rank websites higher if they are updated frequently.

801. Don't include static links to your auctions on your web pages. By static I mean a link that doesn't change automatically. In other words, the burden is on you to take the link down or change it when your sale ends. Are you going to remember to do this? Chances are you won't. Don't make visitors to your website click on links that don't actually take them anywhere.

802. What are the best keywords you can include on your web pages? That depends on your site and what you sell. You can, however, use a free utility called Wordtracker (http://www.wordtracker.com) to suggest keywords based on your site's content.

MARKETING YOUR WEBSITE

803. There's an old-school venue that's still effective for publicizing a website and eBay sales. It's called Usenet. This set of thousands of newsgroups is great, especially if your site and your eBay sales appeal to collectors or enthusiasts in a particular area. Go to the newsgroup and answer questions to promote yourself.

804. Newsgroup and mailing list postings need to have a signature file at the end of each one. The signature file should include your website URL, eBay Store URL, and eBay User ID.

805. Create a business card with your company's name and your website URL as well as your phone number or other contact information. Be sure to include the business card with each of the packages you send out in an effort to increase traffic to your site.

806. Also publicize your website by including the URL in the signature file at the bottom of each email message you send to customers. Include it on your business cards and printed materials, too.

MAKING YOUR WEBSITE CONTENT-RICH

807. Make sure your website contains background information about you, your business, or your merchandise. Such data might not seem directly relevant to making sales, but information sells: it makes you look more knowledgeable, and it turns your website into a resource that shoppers will be more likely to revisit.

808. It's also a good idea to craft a mission statement for your site. This is a one- or two-sentence statement expressing your goals for the site and welcoming people to it.

809. Underneath your mission statement, include a brief bulleted list presenting the types of items you sell on eBay. Each list item can be a link leading to one of the categories in your eBay Store, if you have one.

810. If you include links to your eBay sales descriptions on your About Me page, the links are automatically updated on the fly by eBay. Every time someone visits, the links are gathered at that moment as the page loads. These dynamic links are far better than static links you make on your website.

811. Talking about yourself might seem like a waste of time. But if you make it at least a little relevant to what you buy and sell on eBay, it can help sales. Specifically, tell visitors to your website how long you've been selling, why you like what you do, and why you entered the field. Details like this promote a personal connection that can lead to bids and sales.

812. Be careful with the contact information you publish on your website. Make sure your email address isn't in the body of your web page. You'll get tons of spam. Instead, include a link such as "Questions? <u>Contact</u> me for more information." Make the word Contact a clickable link. In the HTML for your web page, include a mailto link: <a href="mailto:myaddress@mysite.com"> Contact </a>.

813. When you create a website, you give up some privacy. You give eBay members a way to contact you outside of eBay's message system. Be sure to create an email address that is disposable (that you can discard and change when you want more privacy).

814. You can also type your email address in a graphics program, save it in GIF format, crop it tightly, and add it to a web page as a graphic image. That way, visitors will have your web address, and the spammers won't be able to scan it and add it to their mailing lists.

815. You can add a blog to your website using a free tool like Google's Blogger. At the simplest level, a blog gives your customers a chance to know who you are. Knowing something about the human being behind the eBay User ID promotes trust among potential customers, many of whom are reluctant to purchase online.

816. Keep your blog personal but professional. When you sell on eBay and possibly other venues, everything reflects on your business. Realize that your comments will potentially remain online for years. Don't say anything you'll regret later on.

817. By all means, refer to eBay sales in your blog. Make links to your own eBay Store and to eBay resources you use yourself. Use your blog to build your reputation as a knowledgeable eBay seller.

818. Don't be afraid to make links to other web locations on your blog. You can use your blog to promote sellers who are friends of yours. (They can do the same too.)

819. A blog is a commitment. You need to update it at least a few times a week. If you can update your blog once a day, so much the better.

820. You can do all kinds of things with your own website. If you want to sell more effectively on eBay, make sure you link to your eBay sales. The easiest way to make a link is to download some code from the HTML Editor kit (http://affiliates.ebay.com/tools/editor-kit/). The kit enables you to link to your own live sales descriptions and link to them on your web pages.

821. You can also use the Editor Kit to link to someone else's eBay descriptions and display their listings on your website. Why would you want to do this? You can earn between $5 and $13 as an eBay affiliate. If someone clicks on a link you display and eventually makes a Buy It Now purchase or registers as an eBay member, you earn a commission.

822. To become an eBay affiliate, you need to register with the Commission Junction affiliate service. This service keeps tracks of mouse clicks on links you create, and makes sure you get paid if you qualify. Find out more on the eBay Affiliate Welcome page, http://affiliates.ebay.com.

823. If you sell in high volume not only at auction but also through a well-stocked eBay Store, use the Merchant Kit rather than the Editor Kit. The Merchant Kit (http://pages.ebay.com/api/merchantkit.html) gathers links to both your auction sales and your store categories and presents them on a web page.

824. If you don't want to go through the effort of using the Editor Kit, here's an easier way to create links to your current sales: go to your Feedback Profile page (click on your own User ID to get there). In the links on the right-hand side of the page, click Items for Sale. Copy the URL for the page that appears and paste it into the appropriate page on your website.

19.

Working with an Auction Service Provider

eBay sellers tend to be do-it-yourselfers. Their initial tendency is to want to handle everything all by themselves. This is fine up to a point—the point where you realize you're not only exhausted, but you can't grow your business any further on your own. For many sellers, the most effective way to be more productive while still maintaining control of a small-scale eBay business is to sign up with an auction service provider (ASP). An ASP is a company that is in the business of providing software and services especially to entrepreneurs who sell on eBay or other venues, or through their own websites. Their software is designed to streamline the process of listing descriptions and managing sales and customers. Ideally, a good ASP is like your operational business partner, helping you work more efficiently and suggesting new markets. However, many beginning eBay sellers don't know how to begin exploring the world beyond eBay; this chapter will give you some starting points.

825. Locating a storefront in an online shopping area or mall provided by a well-known service like MSN or Yahoo! can gain extra exposure for your business simply because the malls are so well-traveled.

826. Use your online storefront to link to your website, your eBay Store, and your other business "presences." Making links from one site to another not only boosts traffic, it improves your search result placement on Google.

827. Suppose you offer something for sale through eBay and it doesn't sell. After a few weeks, the listing disappears and your work is lost. If you want to relist the item, you have to create the description from scratch. Service providers like Marketworks keep your listings indefinitely so you can relist them anytime.

828. No matter which auction service provider (ASP) you contract with, be aware that you have two kinds of auction management tools you can use. The first is software you install on your computer and that resides on your file system. You have ultimate control over how the software is used, but you use up memory and you have to make sure the software is updated. The second is software you rent as a service using your web browser. The rented service option carries a monthly fee, but doesn't consume memory, and the burden is on the ASP to update the software.

829. If you need to access your auction data and manage your sales from multiple locations and different computers, choose the rented "software as a service" option. If you are most comfortable managing your sales from a single computer, choose the downloaded software option.

830. Some auction management services charge more per month than others, but don't let that be your only criteria for making a decision. The services that are more expensive may, in fact, provide you with a far wider range of tools and resources than you could get otherwise.

ESSENTIAL FEATURES TO LOOK FOR IN AN ASP

831. When you are first starting out, look for software that enables you to list multiple sales. Your first challenge is to streamline the process of designing and listing as many descriptions as possible so you can be more productive.

832. If you have established a business and already have a way to get multiple sales online, look for software that helps you manage your sales and complete transactions. Your primary need is keeping track of where your transactions are and what you need to do at a given time. Additionally, you need to streamline responses to email messages and automate transactions so nothing falls through the cracks.

833. Don't pay too much attention to the amount of photo storage space your ASP gives you. Your average photo should be no more than 25K to 50K in size, so with a relatively small 100MB of space you should be able to store as many as two thousand images. You have free space available to you as part of your Internet access account, so don't pay high fees for extra storage space.

834. Any ASP should provide you with software or services that help you manage email. Email is one of the most time-consuming—and important—activities. The software should help you get email messages out quickly but enable you to personalize them at the same time by adding names, times, and descriptions of what has been purchased.

835. Feedback is often the part of a transaction that gets left until the end, but it's the thing that many buyers want the most. Look for an ASP whose services include feedback automation (most do provide this, actually).

836. A good set of ASP services will include sales analysis. Sales reports will enable you to determine what sells best, what the best times are to sell, and which starting bids work best.

837. Many ASPs will help you print out shipping labels and possibly postage as well. If you can find an ASP that has its services coordinated with one or more of the major shippers, it will save you some trips to the post office.

838. It's hard to keep track of sales tax. One of the nice things of the My eBay/Pay-Pal shipping label service is the fact that sales tax is automatically calculated when the buyer lives in the same state you do. Look for an ASP whose services include sales tax calculation too.

COMBINING AN AUCTION MAN-
AGEMENT SERVICE WITH EBAY
SALES SOFTWARE

839. Start with eBay's sales software. Consider a third-party sales management option when you want a variety of services, such as photo hosting, all in one package. eBay's ProStores (www.prostores.com) is the obvious place to start.

840. If you work with databases all the time, Turbo Lister is a good tool for you, even if you do have a storefront with an auction service provider. You can format sales for Turbo Lister by importing them in CSV format. Choose File, Import From, CSV, and locate the database file you want to import.

841. As you might expect, you can export Turbo Lister data to a CSV file. You can then open it in Excel or another database file. This makes it easy to keep track of your sales and add final sales data.

842. Be sure you export your files before you delete them from Turbo Lister. Turbo Lister only saves sales descriptions. It doesn't track ongoing sales, and it doesn't report final sales prices. My eBay does that.

843. Selling Manager Pro includes a number of features that Blackthorne Manager does not, including inventory management, listing statistics, and automated feedback and post-sales emails.

OTHER SALES MANAGEMENT TOOLS

844. SpareDollar (www.sparedollar.com) is a popular auction management service. The big reason for its popularity is that it's so affordable. For $8.95 a month, you get the ability to create listings, upload listings in bulk, schedule listings in advance for no extra fee, and much more. SpareDollar, at this writing, does not charge insertion fees or commissions on completed sales.

845. SpareDollar, for its $8.95 fee, also provides 50MB of image hosting space. Hosting for images and web pages is one of the most important features you should look for in an auction service provider.

846. It's hard to beat Auctiva (www. auctiva.com) when it comes to price. It's free. You get a listing tool, the ability to create templates called profiles, unlimited image hosting, and even sales reports.

847. One thing Auctiva provides that other auction management services don't is the ability to create an online storefront. All of your eBay auctions and other sales are collected in one place—a web page that you present as your online shop.

848. Vendio (www.vendio.com) is another popular auction management service used by lots of eBay sellers. Vendio's most recognizable service—recognizable because it's seen on lots of auction descriptions—is the Vendio Gallery, a set of images that are taken from a seller's other sales and presented in a moving "filmstrip" format. The basic Gallery service costs $2.95 per month.

849. Vendio also has one of the most robust online storefront solutions among auction service providers. Open a Vendio Store, and your items appear on Google's retail search engine Froogle. You also get search marketing on Yahoo!. The Bronze Store plan costs $4.95 per month plus a Final Value Fee of 1 percent with a maximum of $4.95 per item. The Silver plan costs $9.95 per month plus 20 cents per item sold, and the Gold plan costs $14.95 per month plus 10 cents per item sold.

850. Marketworks (www.marketworks.com) is one of the oldest and most popular auction service providers. Its storefront solution has one notable feature that others don't: you have access to a creative team that helps you design your storefront and gives you guidance on how to make it successful.

851. Simply creating a storefront is one thing. How do you get your inventory into your storefront and replenish it as items are purchased? How do you keep track of inventory so you can make a purchase before you run out? Marketworks links an inventory system to your storefront in order to streamline these "back end" processes.

852. Marketworks also handles another essential feature that you need to consider no matter which service you choose. Shopping comparison sites—like Shopzilla and Shopping.com, which gather the best prices from across the Internet—are terribly popular with consumers, and you need to list your products with them for maximum exposure.

853. ChannelAdvisor (www.channeladvisor. com) also lets you create an e-commerce store. Its ChannelAdvisor Merchant option is linked with PayPal, so customers can pay you there just as they do on eBay.

854. If you are open a store with Chan- nelAdvisor, you are able to list your merchandise on eBay, Overstock.com, and many other marketplaces. You have to call the company to get any information about pricing, however.

855. StoreFront Sales Accelerator for eBay is good if you already use one of the LaGarde, Inc., StoreFront packages, which provide online storefronts with shopping cart technology. This is a $399 add-on for the storefront packages that enables you to place sales listings on eBay. Find out more at www.storefront.net.

856. Truition CMS for eBay (www.truition.com) is a prominent e-commerce storefront service provider, counting Sirius Satellite Radio among its clients. CMS auction lets you create a storefront and list individual items on eBay as well.

857. If this list of auction service providers has you scratching your head, wondering which option is best for you, don't fret. There's a website devoted to auction management software called the Auction Software Review (www.auctionsoftwarereview.com). You'll find services and tools organized by the type of feature you need (Management Solutions, Marketing, Design, Posting, Images, and so on).

858. Do you have sales listings on eBay's overseas sites? You can manage them with a product called Auction Tamer (www.auctiontamer.com). Auction Tamer can also manage sales on Yahoo! and Amazon.com.

859. Mpire (www.mpire.com) offers a variety of auction services for $29.95 per month. One of the nicest feature is its Contact Manager, which keeps track of the real names, User IDs, and contact information for all of your customers.

860. By default, PayPal only presents ten or so of your most recent transactions. Click the tiny link More at the right of the screen to view more transaction results.

861. If you sell vehicles through eBay Motors, you can manage multiple sales, too, through a service called CARad.com (www.carad.com). The service isn't cheap—you pay $9.95 per listing—but you gain the ability to include up to thirty-five photos per description.

862. CARad.com (www.carad.com) is owned by eBay. This listing service is particularly good for auto dealerships; they can pay $299 per month for unlimited listings on eBay Motors.

20.

Boosting Profits

Volume is important when it comes to selling on
eBay. But if you're only making a few cents profit
on each sale, you have to be selling hundreds or
even thousands of items a month to make your
efforts worthwhile. I know one seller who sells
Italian charms, which have a low profit margin;
he's not only very tired, but he's continually looking for new product lines that will give him bigger
profits and reduce the number of sales he has to
complete. You, too, need to evaluate your bottom
line periodically to make sure you're getting your
money's worth for your efforts. Or if you're just
starting out, you need to plan your starting prices
and buy your merchandise with an eye toward
ensuring a profit margin that will keep you going
for the foreseeable future.

863. You're selling, but you're not making a lot of money. How do you ramp things up and become a PowerSeller? One approach: don't try to do everything yourself. Find a service provider or an employee to help you increase volume. (See chapter 19 for suggestions about auction service providers.)

864. Another approach: try strategic philanthropy—holding charity auctions to boost visibility and increase the number of bids you receive, while helping out a worthy cause at the same time.

865. Try to sell seasonal merchandise. Buy and store up summer sports and outdoor equipment during the cold months so you can offer them when the warm weather comes. Buy up holiday decorations in January, when they are inexpensive, and save them up to offer the following November.

866. Branch out from auctions to different selling formats. Some lower-priced or lower-in-demand items sell better at a reasonable fixed price than at an auction with a higher selling price.

867. List fewer items on more days of the week rather than lumping everything on Sunday or one other day. It makes your life easier because you might only have two, three, or four items to ship out on a given night rather than having ten or twelve things to ship out after your one big sales day.

DEVELOP A WINNING ATTITUDE

868. I became a PowerSeller only three months after starting on eBay. How did I do it? I learned from interviewing other PowerSellers that you need to deal in *volume*. You need to start buying in bulk and listing twenty, thirty, or fifty items at a time. Don't limit yourself to selling half a dozen items a week. Try to list half a dozen items four or five nights a week, or every night of the week if you can manage it.

869. Another critical attitude you need to adopt when building volume: lose your fear of spending money and don't be held back by items that don't sell. If something doesn't sell, relist it—or start looking for a more desirable brand. Keep moving forward and don't get discouraged, even when you have one bad sales week. Chances are things will turn around soon.

870. Keep track of your customers. Take the time to record their real names, addresses, User IDs, and what they bought from you. Don't depend on My eBay or PayPal to hold the information for you. PayPal doesn't record customers who pay by check, and My eBay only holds sales data for sixty days.

871. What can you do with those customer names and details that can make you more productive? You can market directly to them. I have one shoe customer who wears an unusual size: 14A. Good shoes are hard to find for him. Whenever I find a pair in his size, I send him an email and a photo. I've sold two other pairs of shoes that way.

SELLER CENTRAL RESOURCES

872. Check out the newsletters in the Seller Central area (pages.ebay.com/sellercentral) for suggestions of seasonal and holiday-related merchandise that tends to sell well and that you should purchase any time of year.

873. The Advanced Selling area of Seller Central contains some useful links to eBay sales tools, which will speed up your listings. You'll also find a link to the eBay Reseller Marketplace, a place where you can find wholesale sellers. It's specially designed for eBay sellers who want to buy merchandise on eBay that they can resell on eBay.

874. You'll also find a link to the Wholesale Lots area of eBay. In theory, this is supposed to be a place where eBay sellers can find wholesale merchandise to sell, but most sellers I've interviewed tell me it's hard to find bargains there.

875. Buried near the bottom of the Advanced Selling page of Seller Central is a link to a useful e-booklet entitled 7 Steps to Scalability. It's a very focused, no-frills action plan designed to help people just like you increase their sales on eBay. The direct URL is pages.ebay.com/advancedsellingguide/advancedsellingguide.pdf.

876. Chances are you're a lone entrepreneur, or you have a skeleton crew. How do you compete with the big box, brick-and-mortar stores? One way is to focus on unusual, hard-to-find, offbeat merchandise that the big chain stores just don't carry. Another is to provide personal service the big stores don't match—calling buyers on the phone to verify orders, sending personal notes, and the like.

877. For certain items such as consumer electronics components, it makes sense to offer a warranty. If you sell in eBay's Consumer Electronics category, you can offer one. Find out more at pages.ebay.com/help/warranty/seller_overview.html.

SEVEN WAYS TO INCREASE PRODUCTIVITY

878. One surefire way to increase your eBay revenues is to become an authorized dealer for a line of well-known products. This requires a good deal of legwork—you need to contact the company, explain who you are and what you want to do, and provide them with evidence that indicates you are a reputable seller. Partnerships with companies such as EG, Disney, and Sun increase the Average Sale price, which is a key metric in determining eBay's transaction fees.

879. What do you do with all of that excess stock you can't sell on eBay? You can automatically export your Unsold Items to a site called iOffer (www.ioffer.com) using a software tool called Mr. Grabber. Then you list your merchandise and have shoppers make you an offer.

880. When you get really big and really successful, consider what one successful eBay Titanium PowerSeller named Dallas Golf (www.dallasgolf.com) does. The company buys merchandise from its competitors and resells it for a profit. It came up with a trade-in feature that allows other golf dealers and individuals to calculate a trade-in price.

881. Dallas Golf's Chris Smith says that many sellers fall short simply because they don't try to sell all the inventory they have. Look around at your leftover items and put them up for sale on your eBay Store or on Overstock or iOffer. If you don't at least give yourself a chance to succeed, you never will.

882. Donate a percentage of each auction sale to charity. You can do so from eBay's Sell Your Item form. Sellers who do this tell me that they get more bids for their items, and more attention in general. Not only that, but it's a good thing to do, too.

883. Consider opening a drop-off store in your area to increase your sales volume and come up with a regular source of merchandise to sell on eBay. If you already have some retail experience, you can open your own independent store. If not, consider signing up with one of the drop-off store franchises that can give you a jump start.

884. There's a free accounting tool available to you if you run an eBay Store, or if you use the selling tools Selling Manager, Selling Manager Pro, or Blackthorne Basic and Pro. It's called Accounting Assistant, and it will export your sales data to QuickBooks or Simple Start.

USING SALES RESEARCH TOOLS

885. When you sign up with an auction service provider, you receive many benefits beyond a storefront. For instance, Andale (http://www.andale.com) includes an Andale Research tool. The tool presents you with a detailed study—including charts and graphs—of the performance of completed items. It's available for $7.95 per month by itself or in packages with other sales tools.

886. When do shoppers visit your eBay Store? The Page Views Report tracks the number of visits to a particular page over time. If you get the most visits on a Sunday, try to have your auction sales end on that day. On the other hand, if your second most popular day is Thursday, you might want to schedule more auction sales to end on that day.

887. The Visits Report is also part of the basic eBay Sales Reports package. It gives you a rough idea of the total number of visitors to your site over time. The Unique Visitors report is better. It tells you how many different visitors you have. If someone viewed a page twenty times in the same day, it only counts as one unique visit.

888. If you don't own an eBay Featured or Anchor Store, how can you track and analyze visits to your website? Sellathon (www.sellathon.com) has a tool called View-Tracker that is used by many sellers. The basic package costs $4.95 per month, and a thirty-day free trial is available.

ENCOURAGING REPEAT BUSINESS

889. Repeat customers are the key to any successful business. Write down a list of customers and what they're looking for. Ask if they need any other items after you make the sale. When you find something they want, contact them directly.

890. When someone buys something from you a second or third time, it is very gratifying. Include a little extra gift in your package to reward your repeat customers and encourage them to come back again.

891. When you send out an eBay invoice, there is a small box that lets you send a note to the customer. You might use this note to briefly suggest other items you have that they might be interested in.

892. Even better than the note on the invoice is a sheet you add to your box when you ship an item that has been purchased. Make the list of items targeted: pick sizes or styles that complement what was just purchased and that the buyer is likely to want. Don't send a list of purses to a male customer; come up with things that are targeted toward him.

893. You have one more chance to upsell to current customers after you pack the box. If you ship with My eBay and the U.S. Postal Service, you have the chance to send a note when you purchase postage. Send this note: tell people their package is coming, and urge them to look at other items you have that they might be interested in.

21.

Strategic Purchasing for Your eBay Business

The savvy eBay businessperson is constantly on the lookout for new merchandise. He doesn't sit back and rest on his laurels. You always have to look for new things to sell, as tastes and times change. Some of your purchasing might be on eBay; other purchases might be done on Amazon.com or Overstock.com. The key is to keep looking for sources of merchandise that eBay shoppers will want to buy and that you can resell for a profit. As every eBay seller knows, that's easier said than done, but the tips presented in this chapter will point you in the right direction.

CREATING A PURCHASING SCHEDULE

894. Come up with a plan for purchasing several times a year. You might plan to make strategic purchases on a quarterly basis, or twice a year. It is important to set up an annual budget that allocates money for seasonal purchases. Not only do you need to have resources available for making purchases, but this also helps you to know when you're likely to have an influx of income so you can plan to meet your personal needs.

895. Knowing when your busy times will be also helps you allocate space in your storage areas for accommodating your inventory. Many sellers have to clean or restore the items that they will then resell. If you deal with larger items, you may have to rent storage space or set up areas in your warehouse when you are likely to be fully stocked.

896. Get in the habit of purchasing in advance for seasons and events coming up later in the year. Some of it might depend on weather, if you deal with goods that are more usable when the temperatures are hotter or cooler. There are also plenty of holidays that are geared to acquiring gifts or decorations. A smart seller is eager to pitch her wares when a large audience is likely to be eager to purchase.

897. Once you have determined how frequently you want to sell, come up with a plan. If you plan to purchase on a quarterly basis, come up with a review of the previous quarter. Your quarter review should include the value of your inventory, your gross sales revenue, and the total number of items you ended up selling below your desired price.

898. If you sell many different items in various categories, simplify your planning. Focus on one major category at a time. You'll give yourself less work to do, and you will be able to isolate successful categories from failing ones.

899. A major goal of this planning exercise is determining how often your inventory is exhausted and when you need to make a new purchasing effort. While some eBay sellers purchase constantly, after you've been at it a while you get tired of the constant shopping and look forward to only having to purchase at certain predetermined times.

900. For most eBay sellers, it makes sense to purchase based on season. Think about Fall/Holidays (October–December), Winter Doldrums (January–March), Spring Rebirth (April–June), and Summer Slowdown (July–September).

SEARCHING FOR THE LOWEST PRICES

901. Froogle (froogle.google.com) lets you search through an extensive database of online retailers, and sorts results by price. You stand a good chance of finding a competitive price if you start here.

902. Other web-based shopping services, such as PriceGrabber.com (www.pricegrabber.com), collect online prices. The results include shipping costs.

903. When you become a PowerSeller and start purchasing in quantity, you are often confronted with major purchasing decisions. Should you buy ten thousand pairs of shoes at a certain price? Use eBay to do market research. Are there a lot of these shoes being sold? There should be. A brand that is well-known and desirable will probably have been sold on eBay sometime in the past two weeks. If you don't see any items after doing both a current search and Completed Items search, be skeptical.

904. What sorts of starting prices and Buy It Now prices are being offered on eBay for the items you want to purchase? The prices should be higher than what you would have to pay for your purchase. If things go the other way around—your prospective purchase price is higher than the starting bids—you'd better negotiate another deal, or look for another one elsewhere.

905. A tool called Pluck Auction Scout (www.pluck.com) can be used to search eBay not once, but constantly. The tool looks for items in a particular category. You can use it to monitor what sales are ending at any particular time and what kinds of merchandise are fetching the best prices.

906. When you research completed auctions looking for items to purchase, pay attention to the sell-through rate (STR). How many items like the ones you are thinking of purchasing are up for sale? How many of those actually sell? If you find that fifty were for sale and only ten sold, that's an STR of 50/10 or 20 percent, which isn't so good. Good STRs vary from category to category, but in the clothing area, you should get 50 percent or better.

907. Look through some well-known eBay Stores for the brands you want to buy. Hopefully some items with those brands have been sold recently. Do the stores from which the items were sold consistently put those same items online on a weekly basis? If you find that a few were sold one week and none were put online for several weeks, steer clear of those brands. They're probably not desirable.

ANALYZE YOUR COMPETITION

908. Use the research software included with HammerTap (www.hammer tap.com) to scan lists of the Top 10 and Bottom 10 sellers in a particular category. What constitutes success in that category? What constitutes failure? Reviewing the data can help you make informed evaluations.

909. Once you choose a category and come up with a system for making sales, it's easy to get stuck in a rut. Instead, keep an eye on the competition. Use Terapeak's seller lists to track what others are doing in the same category. Find out what products and models they're selling, to see if there's anything you are missing.

910. Also pay attention to the kinds of sales your competitors are using. Do they mostly use auction sales or Buy It Now sales? Which types of sales give the best results?

911. Scan the listings of the top sellers in your category. (You'll find some suggestions in the following chapter for how to search for your main competitors.) What sorts of sales policies do they have? Do they accept PayPal or other services? How much do they charge for shipping? Do they let the customer calculate shipping?

912. After I had been selling on eBay for several months, I got to recognize certain User IDs. There were people who consistently bid on my shoes but did not win. Others won and came back to bid on other sales. I was happy to see the repeat business, and even purchased some items with regular customers in mind.

913. Stalking has a bad reputation in the real world, but there's nothing wrong with doing some active research as an eBay seller. You can even take it a step further and shadow your customers to see where else they shopped and bid. You do this by searching By Seller in the Advanced Search area.

914. Go to eBay's Wholesale Lots area. Do a Completed Items search for lots of the kinds of the items you sell. Who buys those lots consistently? Go back to eBay to see if those same members resell their merchandise in smaller lots. There's no guarantee you'll find them. But if you do, you'll have a clue to how your competition operates.

915. Just like an intersection that has a gas station on each of its corners, sometimes collaboration among competitors can lead to mutual advantage. There are many methods to discover ways to acquire your merchandise, and getting that knowledge directly from the horse's mouth is certainly a credible concept.

916. It pays to learn from the best. Many of the top sellers on eBay are members of the Professional eBay Sellers Alliance. To become a member of PESA, you have to be a very active and successful seller. (Requirements are described in detail at http://www.gopesa.org/pes_membership.cfm.) But you can still learn from PESA members. You can join the PESA mailing list and read publications on http://www.gopesa.org, the group's website.

917. Another service, Glinos (glinos.is-a-geek.com:63125.cgi-bin/total.html) tracks the top twenty eBay sellers not by sales volume but by the amount of feedback they get. It can give you a rough idea of the top sellers on the site—or at least the most active sellers—at a given time.

TIPS FOR SAVVY SEARCHING

918. The search box you see at the top of every page is just the beginning. You can refine searches in order to come up with items you can resell online. The first step is to click on the Advanced Search link or go directly to http://search.ebay.com/ws/search/AdvSearch.

919. Once you do a search, you can enlarge it by browsing through categories. When you get a set of search results, eBay presents you with the link Matching Categories on the left-hand side of the page. Click the category name to go to its opening page. When you browse this category, you might turn up some items that don't otherwise turn up in search results.

920. The Advanced Search page isn't the only way to search eBay's database. If you want faster and more sophisticated searches, try My Auction Search (www.myauctionsearch.com). It lets you run as many as ten searches at the same time and search Half.com and other areas of eBay from a single interface.

921. The simplest way to focus a search is to limit it to a single category. Go to Advanced Search and choose the most likely category. Suppose you're looking for a cell phone. If you do a search for "cell phone" in the basic eBay Search box at this writing, you come up with no less than 113,687 items. If you limit your search to the Cell Phones category, you get 100,000. Well, it's a start! Choose the Phones Only section, and you get 4,818 results. Choose Phones with New Plan Purchase, and you get only 262 results.

922. If you don't find what you're looking for the first time, redo the search after checking the Search title and description box. This doesn't limit the search—it enlarges the number of results. Scan those results, and you might find a few sales you missed the first time. They might be just the bargains you're looking for—the results are in the body of the description and not the title, so most bidders will miss them.

923. The Idea Manifesto was written in 2001, but it's still full of useful approaches with regard to searching on eBay. You'll find it at www.timeblaster.com/support_top_10_secrets.shtml.

924. Type more than one word in the search box—but avoid words like "and" and "or." Auction results will only include descriptions with all of the words in the title. "Wilson Golf Clubs" will return fewer items than "Golf Clubs," for instance.

925. Quotation marks tell the search engine to search for an exact combination of words. But what if you are looking for an especially popular item? In that case, searching for an exact brand name or model number can focus your search to exactly the object you want.

926. Sometimes the fact that you find nothing when you do a search on eBay is also useful information. Sometimes, despite searching every which way, no results will show up. When this happens, at least you'll know that no such items exist in eBay's database.

927. The Search Options box contains a variety of options that can limit your searches. Suppose you want to do a test to see how popular PayPal is among your competition. Search for one of the items you're offering yourself. Then, after the results appear, check Items listed with PayPal, and click Show Items. You can then count the number of PayPal results and compare them to the original results.

928. Suppose you want to set a Buy It Now price for an item you're selling, and you want to do a survey of similar items that are currently being sold on eBay. Check the Buy It Now Items box under Search Options, and then click Show Items.

929. Does any one of your competitors offer Express Mail as an option? If they do, and you only offer Priority Mail, you may be losing business. Search for something you are offering, check Get It Fast under Search Options, and click Show Items. You'll see just how popular Express Mail is as an option.

930. Gift Items are those that include gift wrapping and possibly even a card with your package. Do many of your competitors offer this? If they do, you should consider it. Do a search in Search Options. Check the Gift Items box and search for something you're selling. It might be revealing to see how many other sellers are offering Gift Items.

931. Are other items up for sale on eBay priced anywhere near your own? To find out, search for one of your own items and enter a price range in the Items Priced boxes under Search Options.

932. Don't overlook the unobtrusive link <u>Customize</u> in the phrase "<u>Customize</u> options displayed above" at the bottom of Search Options. Click it, and you can add and subtract the items you need most from the Search Options list. As long as you're logged in with the same User ID, your preferences will remain the next time you do a search on eBay.

933. One of the best search options—and one that doesn't show up by default—is Number of Bids. Use it to find items that have attracted ten to twenty bids on All Categories of eBay. These are items that are particularly hot, and you should try to sell them yourself.

934. Here's a way to find really popular brands in your own area. Suppose you sell antiques. Go to the Antiques category. Enter the word antique in the search box. Specify only items with ten to thirty bids. Click Show Items in the Search Options column. You'll come up with really popular items that are currently selling in this category.

935. Sunday is the most popular day to end sales. Do the ten-to-thirty-bid test on a Sunday, and you'll get more meaningful search results.

SEARCH FOR YOUR COMPETITORS

936. How many eBay sellers in your category use the Best Offer option? Customize the Search Options box by adding Best Offer to the Options displayed. Do a search for one of your own items, check the Best Offer option, and click Show Items.

937. How many of your eBay Store items are included in other people's stores? To search the competition, add the Store Inventory Items option to Search Options, check that option, and click Show Items.

938. What are the most popular and biggest eBay Stores in your area? Do a search for anything you tend to sell regularly. Check the See All Matching Stores link. It's located under More on eBay on the left-hand side of the search results. You'll come up with a list of stores, arranged by the number of items they have for sale. In my own area (shoes) I have Gotham City Online, Gravevinehill, and ShoeMetro near the top of the list.

939. Once you search for your big competitors and identify them, don't be intimidated by how many things they have for sale. They *have* to sell a lot in order to cover expenses. You can compete by being selective and selling one-of-a-kind or hard-to-find items the big players don't carry.

940. Keep in mind that many folks drive past huge malls and discount stores to shop at a mom-and-pop store. It is there that they feel most at home. They are willing to pay extra for special services or individual attention. As an eBay seller, you should also try to promote a welcoming spirit that bigger stores don't offer and attract those who are looking for that personal touch that means so much.

941. Once you find some competitors, you can save them as Favorites. Make note of their User IDs. Go to My eBay, and click Sellers under All Favorites. Click Add a New Seller or Store. Enter the User ID, add a note if needed, and then click Save Seller/Store.

SPECIAL SEARCH TERMS

942. If you don't know how to spell an entire word, use an asterisk (*), which serves as a wild card symbol. A search for *Pors** will turn up lots of items having to do with the motor car company Porsche, if you can't remember how to spell it. But you'll also come up with many other search terms, such as Porsgrund, which is a manufacturer of plates.

943. Use the minus sign (-) if you want to eliminate something from search results. For instance, if you want to find all the items on eBay that have *Pors* in the title but not the word Porsche, type the following: *Pors* -Porsche*. In that case, you'll really come up with lots and lots of Porsgrund plates.

944. The minus sign comes in handy if you are looking for misspelled items. These are items that won't show up on search results and that are likely to have few bidders. You might find some real bargains here. If you search for *Pors* -Porsche*, for instance, you come up with Porshe and many other misspelled Porsche items.

945. Misspellings are like gold to a buyer who wants bargains. If you are aware of common misspellings of items in your field, search for those misspellings. If you find one, you might end up being the only bidder.

946. Resist the temptation to email a seller and tell her about a misspelling. It might irritate and embarrass her. It might also provide you with bidding competition you don't necessarily want.

947. If you have two spellings you want to search for (such as Porsche and Porshe), use both of them in the search box. Separate them with a comma, but do not put a blank space between them: *Porsche,porshe*.

948. You can combine the minus sign with a set of two or more words. Put the words you want to exclude in parentheses and you will prevent them from showing up: *Porsh -(Porsche,Porshe)* will only present titles with Porsh in the search results, for instance.

949. If you take away the minus sign and include two or more words in parentheses, you include them in the search results. This is commonly done to search for variations on a group of words such as Teddy Boys and Teddy Bears. *Teddy (boys,bears)* would present both phrases, for instance.

950. Once you construct an elaborate search, you need to conduct it periodically, say, once every couple of weeks or once a month. That way you'll get a picture of how the marketplace shifts as the seasons change and people need or want different items.

951. Save your search as a Favorite. Click Add to Favorite Searches, which appears at the top of a list of search results. You can then access your favorite searches from the All Favorites section of My eBay.

OTHER SEARCH SERVICES

952. If eBay's search results are inadequate, try Terapeak's eBay Marketplace Research tool. It's called Smart Buyer, and you find it on the site's home page (www.terapeak.com). It gives you live search results, just like eBay, but you also get an average price that eBay doesn't provide.

953. If you want three months of eBay past sales listings, along with studies of sales trends, sign up for Terapeak's search service. You get a fourteen-day free trial, and only have to pay $9.95 per month for the Lite service. (A more full-featured version costs $14.95 per month.)

954. Abidia provides wireless searching of eBay's Completed Items database. It's available for many cell phones and wireless services for $4.99 per month or a one-time $39.99 fee. It's available for the Treo Smartphone, BlackBerry devices, and other Palm-powered devices.

955. Andale (www.andale.com) offers a service called Andale Research for $7.95 per month. It reports on average sales prices and lets you compare eBay prices to those on Froogle and other sites.

956. Suppose you want to buy a set of golf clubs you can then resell. Do a search for the brand and model numbers in the usual eBay search box. When the search box appears, make note of the number of sellers who are offering the same item. This is your competition. Evaluate their feedback numbers and the number of bids to see if you can really expect to sell your item while competing with them.

957. In the search results that appear after you do a conventional search, research completed transactions and sale prices. Check the Search Options box on the left side of the search results page. Check the Completed listings box. Then click Show Items to review completed transactions in the past two or three weeks.

958. When you are reviewing many pages worth of search results, you need to save time. Click the Price heading to sort items by price. You'll probably want to click Price two times. The first time, it sorts by lowest price first. It's more revealing to click Price again and review the highest prices paid for the specified item, however.

22.

Miscellaneous Tips and Strategies

eBay is a rich environment that many of us have spent years exploring. And no matter how long you've been on eBay (or writing about it, in my case), there are always new things to discover. Some tips and tricks don't fit into any of the preceding chapters. I've gathered them here in a catch-all chapter. That doesn't mean they're afterthoughts, by any means; you'll find some of the most useful and unique ideas here for improving your eBay sales activities.

959. Looking for some sweet inspiration? Reading the success story of another seller never fails to brighten my day. Sometimes I even get a good idea for my own business. Not being shy to toot its own horn, eBay tells tales of how it has changed people's lives in its newsletter, the Chatter, at pages.ebay.com/community/chatter/index.html.

960. Many eBay sellers have multiple accounts, each with a different User ID. Why, you ask? They use one ID for selling and one for buying. Having a different ID for buying helps them go incognito so other buyers don't get the idea that an item is highly desirable or a good buy. Different IDs also enable sellers to complain on the discussion boards without drawing undue attention to themselves.

961. Often, you run into styrofoam that has been molded to fit around a stereo receiver or other item. Don't throw it out; break it up by hand into smaller pieces, and use it as packing material in your shipments.

962. You might get your listing fee refunded if eBay goes offline when your sale is running. eBay's policy is to extend auctions for an extra twenty-four hours if sales are interrupted by a hard outage, meaning two or more hours.

GATHERING IMPORTANT BUSINESS INFORMATION

963. An informed seller is an effective seller. Take the time to read the site's Help files, and subscribe to the eBay Group Announcement Board (groups.ebay.com/forum.jspa?forumID=1072) to learn about new promotions and programs. Nobody has time to participate in every single opportunity available, but just learning what's available helps you keep your finger on the pulse of your trade.

964. Rules and regulations can be annoying, but it's important that you follow proper procedures. Not only will noncompliance make you work less efficiently and possibly lead to negative feedback, but it undermines the entire system. You should read eBay's User Agreement (pics.ebaystatic.com/aw/pics/services/eBayPolicies/yeuaSubHdr_285x40.gif) at least once so you know what's expected of you.

965. Be sure that, at some point, you review the list of problems that constitute seller noncompliance at pages.ebay.com/help/policies/seller-non-performance.html?ssPageName=CMDV:AB. That's a good way to know about a trouble spot without suffering the consequences on your own. As with the rest of life, it's a good thing as an eBay seller to learn from the mistakes of others.

966. Don't assume that a fact that you knew yesterday will be true tomorrow. The economy keeps changing. Trends and fashions come and go. To keep up with your competition, you have to know which way the wind is blowing. You can do it right on eBay, by scanning the What's Hot lists in Seller Central and the lists of popular search terms (buy.ebay.com).

967. Knowing something about the ideas behind eBay will give you an idea about how to conduct your own business activities here—and eBay will even begin to function much like your business partner. It has been said that a genius perceives the obvious that nobody else sees. Information sponsored by eBay is available to one and all. But it's how you process and use that information that makes you more powerful and successful.

968. Finding a steady stream of wholesale merchandise is important. However, one-of-a-kind collectibles have far less competition, and can help you stand out from the crowd. Try for a balance of both types of sales items.

969. While you don't want to give away all of your trade secrets, you don't want to be totally isolated, either. Collaborate with your friends and colleagues on the eBay Community forums (http://hub.ebay.com/community). There's nothing wrong with comparing notes with your competitors, either. PowerSellers compare notes and learn from one another all the time.

TIME MANAGEMENT

970. Don't focus too much on scheduling. Sundays are generally the best days to end a sale, but spread out your activities over the entire week to build volume. That also saves you from spending most of your time every Monday packing and shipping.

971. Find time for your family. eBay can quickly consume all of your free time—and your boxes and shelves full of merchandise have a tendency to consume your living space, too. Carve out a few hours in the day for dinner with your spouse and kids. Try to involve your family in your business. If they're willing helpers, packing and organizing can be a great way to bring everyone in the family together.

972. Some disasters are unpredictable, but other times you can get a heads-up when eBay is scheduled to be offline. Your sales probably wouldn't be ending in the early morning hours when scheduled interruptions for service usually take place. But it pays to find out about any scheduled interruptions, as well as other recent service problems, on the System Status Announcement Board, www2.ebay.com/aw/announce.shtml.

MASTERING THE FEEDBACK SYSTEM

973. Often, people have to remind one another to leave feedback. (In fact, I have to be reminded to do this pretty regularly.) Make the reminder when you send a note out to your customers to let them know that their package is in the mail. There's a space for a personal message when you print shipping labels through My eBay and PayPal; take advantage of it and remind buyers to leave feedback after their item arrives.

974. Study the feedback comments left by buyers for PowerSellers in your sales category who have high feedback numbers. See if you can judge for yourself what impresses buyers. It may be quick delivery, it may be good packaging, it may be a willingness to address special requests, or all of the above. Whatever it is, try to emulate it yourself.

975. Experienced sellers—especially those who depend on eBay sales for a regular source of income—often turn to instruction to make some extra money. They become teachers at local community colleges, telling their neighbors how to buy and sell on eBay. It's a great way to build your visibility and make new contacts as well.

976. eBay's own workshops (http://pages.ebay.com/community/workshopcalendar/current.html) are among the best sources of information when it comes to learning specific aspects of buying or selling on the site. Often, sessions are conducted by eBay sellers themselves. Browse through the archives of past workshop sessions to find a topic that interests you.

977. Leave feedback for multiple users quickly. Yes, it's nice to type a separate personalized comment for each person with whom you've done business. Type a standard comment such as "Great buyer; good communication; would sell to this person again." Save it in a word processing program. Copy it, and go to your feedback page. Click Leave Feedback, and you'll see a list of all the people you need to leave feedback for. Paste the comment in each box, then click Leave Feedback to leave all the comments at once.

978. Before you give blanket feedback comments to everyone on your feedback list, take a moment and think. Do some of those people have yet to pay for their items? Did you just send out the items? You don't want to leave feedback for a buyer who has yet to complete the transaction. Many sellers only leave feedback for people who have left feedback for *them*. Consider following this example yourself.

979. Don't overuse negative feedback. Too many people leave negative feedback if they're impatient with slow delivery or careless packing. Negative feedback should be saved until something goes really wrong: a buyer fails to pay, or a seller fails to deliver. Otherwise, negative feedback becomes meaningless.

980. Don't forget that you can leave neutral feedback under the right circumstances. Typically, neutral feedback is used if a buyer doesn't follow your terms of sale and pays with a form of payment you don't accept, if an item is packed poorly, or if delivery is slow.

981. When you are trying to avoid negative feedback (and sellers are always trying to avoid it), observe the general rules of netiquette that have applied on the Internet since its earliest days. Respond quickly and without resorting to abusive language, write in complete sentences, be patient, and avoid getting angry—even if someone sends you a message that really aggravates you.

982. Remember not to use feedback as a means to coerce someone. For example: "If you don't leave positive feedback for me, I'll leave negative feedback for you," or "If you complain about my merchandise, I'll leave you negative feedback." eBay will end your listing and possibly cancel your account if you are found to have engaged in such behavior.

983. Feedback comments can be difficult to search, especially when a buyer or seller has thousands of individual comments. Go to the Feedback Forum page (pages.ebay.com/services/forum/feedback.html), enter the member's User ID, and press Enter. When the user's feedback page appears, scroll to the bottom and choose the largest number available (200) from the Items per page drop-down list. Click Ctrl+F to open your browser's Find dialog box. Scroll quickly down the page, scanning for the bright red minus icon that denotes a negative comment. This is time-consuming, but seeing all feedback comments in chronological order lets you know if negative comments have been left during a recent day, week, or month.

984. A German language site, Toolhaus.org (http://www.toolhaus.org), contains a number of search utilities that you can use for free. You can search for negative feedback left for a seller, see what the feedback says, and more.

985. If someone from overseas makes a purchase from you and you want to leave feedback, it's an extra-nice touch to leave it in the member's native language. Go to Babelfish (babelfish.altavista.com) and translate it. But keep your comments simple—you can't depend on Babelfish to make a 100 percent accurate translation.

986. There are simple things to avoid receiving any kind of negative feedback from your buyers. For example, communicate with them quickly at every step of the transaction. In many cases what you say isn't so important as the fact that you responded politely and completely.

987. Another tactic is to encourage your buyers to email you with any questions or complaints *before* they leave feedback. That will give you a chance to straighten out misunderstandings or otherwise to make things right without a problem affecting your all-important ratings.

988. If there's something you don't like about your feedback, or if there's something you think is misleading about your feedback to other eBay members, you do have the option of making your feedback private. When you do this, only you can see your feedback. It defeats the purpose of the trust system on eBay, and is likely to engender mistrust among your customers. But you should be aware that it is available as an option. To make your feedback private, go to feedback.ebay.com/ws/eBayISAPI.dll?Feedback Option, check the button next to Make my profile private, and click Submit.

989. Before you decide to make your feedback private, consider responding to feedback that other members leave that you don't agree with. Go to your feedback profile and click Respond next to the comment. Take care not to be abusive or angry, or you'll just inspire a counter-response, and all of your customers will have the chance to view a virtual argument between you and the other party.

990. If you had to leave negative feedback for another member and that person rectified the problem (for example, the person paid for what was purchased), be sure to leave a follow-up comment that appears beneath your original comment. It's just common courtesy, and it helps clean up the other member's profile.

991. Can you remove feedback from your list of comments? Not entirely. However, you can turn to the mediation services of SquareTrade (http://www.squaretrade.com) to have your comments withdrawn. Withdrawal can only take place under certain circumstances. You have to file a case, and work with a Mediator to attempt to work out the dispute with the member who left the feedback. If feedback is withdrawn, it doesn't count in your feedback rating. But the original comment remains in the Feedback Forum.

TAXES AND ACCOUNTING

992. Don't forget, you need to collect sales tax from buyers who live in the same state where you reside (unless you live in one of the handful of states that doesn't collect sales tax at all, of course). When tax time comes, you need to report your taxes to your state's department of revenue, too. If you collect payments through My eBay and PayPal, sales tax is calculated automatically for you and added to the invoices that are sent to your customers.

993. When you set up a business for yourself, whether it's a sole proprietorship or a corporation, you need professional help. A qualified tax accountant can help you set up deductions, depreciate equipment, and create a schedule by which you need to pay your taxes. The hundred or two hundred dollars you might pay for an accountant are more than made up by your savings in taxes and penalties.

994. Be aware of when you need to pay your taxes. April 15 may not be the only tax deadline you need to observe. You need to pay an estimated tax on a quarterly basis when you're in business for yourself, and report business profits or losses.

995. Keep detailed books of your sales data. Don't depend on eBay to be your only source of records. Create a database or a table in a word processing document in which you record sale prices, purchase prices, and other expenses. Make sure you record sales tax, any payroll expenses, your gross profit margin, and descriptions of the items you sell.

996. One of the best kinds of financial records you can keep is a balance sheet. This tracks your assets and your liabilities, and your income and expenses. On the one side, you have your equipment and inventory, your cash on hand, and your other assets. On the other side, you record expenses, bills to pay, sales tax, payroll, and other liabilities.

997. Be sure you keep backups of your computerized records. Even if you only print out your records once in a while and stuff them in an envelope, this is better than nothing. Also back up the data from your PayPal account. Copy the data to a CD periodically; you can fit several years worth of data on a single disk.

998. Computerized records kept on eBay and PayPal aren't permanent unless you can save them. Be sure you keep all the paper records you have that demonstrate how much you've paid for supplies and inventory. These include credit card bills, paper receipts, canceled checks, and bank statements.

HEADING OFF TROUBLE BEFORE IT OCCURS

999. If you are delayed in shipping because you were out of town, make up for it by sending a preemptive email. Before the customer complains, quickly send out a message like the following: "I was called out of town for a few days and wasn't here when your payment arrived. I've tried to make up for the delay by sending your package Express Mail. I'm sorry for the inconvenience."

1000. Suppose you discover something when packing up the item that you didn't notice when you first described it. It happens all the time: a crack, a scratch, or a blemish shows up that throws you into a panic. Take a photo of the flaw and send it to the buyer along with the following message: "I was very surprised to discover a scratch in your shoes that I didn't notice before. I've taken a photo and am sending it to you now. If you no longer want the shoes, I understand; I'll refund your money right away. Otherwise, let me know and I'll ship out to you as soon as possible."

Appendix A:
Resources for Sellers

I've written a number of books about eBay in which I present a more-or-less comprehensive roundup of resources for buyers and sellers on the site. In this book, I've made an effort to present tips that come from my own experience. I'd like to do the same in this appendix. I'm listing resources that I either know and have used personally or that other sellers have recommended to me.

EBAY RESOURCES

My eBay
Click the My eBay button in the navigation bar. You need to know about My eBay. Even if you eventually decide to use another sales management tool, you'll still need to connect to this page periodically to change your preferences. You can

revise your listings or relist items easily from this page, too.

Reviews & Guides
reviews.ebay.com
I'm impressed with the quality of the reviews on eBay. It's not surprising; they're written by eBay buyers and sellers who know what they're talking about. They volunteer to write the reviews, so they want to share information with other members.

eBay Stores
stores.ebay.com
There was a lot of complaining when eBay raised its Basic Store fee to $15.95 per month, but that means you only need to sell one or two items from your store each month to at least break even. A store is a convenient place to list an item when someone asks you to purchase it. Plus, it only costs a few cents to place a description there. I still think stores are worthwhile.

Popular Searches
keyword.ebay.com
It's fascinating to be able to learn in seconds what the most popular keyword searches are on eBay. Even better, you can drill down into your category and subcategory of choice to see what people are looking for most often.

SERVICE PROVIDERS

Terapeak
www.terapeak.com
Yes, you have to pay a monthly fee ($9.95 per month for the Lite version, and $16.95 per month for the Complete version) for Terapeak's search service. Yes, they promote themselves heavily to people like me who cover the industry. But the fact is that they have a useful product, and they fill a need that eBay doesn't.

WEBSITE UTILITIES

Macromedia Dreamweaver
www.dreamweaver.com
I wrote a whole book on Dreamweaver, so it would probably be surprising if I didn't recommend it personally. The program will do everything you could possibly ask of a web editor: you can make the same change on all pages at once, and you can create "rollovers" and other special effects. The only problem is that the new version, MX, is expensive at $399 and consumes lots of computer memory (256MB RAM, 650MB of hard disk space).

Mozilla Composer
www.mozilla.org
If you want to create a simple web page and you don't want to spend a lot of money—or any money at all, for that matter—download the free web browser suite Mozilla, which includes a built-in web page creation tool. It's easy to use, it lets you create tables, and makes it easy to format text and insert photos.

Google Web Directory

Google is one of the most exciting sets of web services around. At the very least, you should register your store's name and URL in the Google Web directory (www.google.com/addurl.html) so you can be listed along with other web-based businesses.

GRAPHICS TOOLS

CoolText

www.cooltext.com

I've used it, it works, and it's a great online service. And it's free. You can create your own using a free online utility such as Cool Text (www.cooltext.com), or you can hire a graphic designer and get a high-quality logo for less than $500. You can use it for years to come on your stationery and business cards as well as your web page, so it's well worth the investment.

Paint Shop Pro

www.corel.com

When you need to adjust colors, crop images, or simply brighten an image, you don't need a complex application like Adobe Photoshop. This tried-and-true graphics program will do everything you need, and it only costs $99.

Adobe Photoshop Elements

http://www.adobe.com/digitalimag/main.html

Having written a book about this program, it would be surprising if I didn't recommend it personally. At only $99, Photoshop Elements is the little brother of the big, powerful application called

Adobe Photoshop. Photoshop Elements is designed specifically for working with photos. There are great utilities for sharpening images; there is one built-in feature that lets you view several variations on a photo so you can choose the version on you want.

AuctionBytes

www.auctionbytes.com

The fact that I write columns occasionally for this useful website doesn't influence my opinion of it. I used to visit AuctionBytes plenty of times before I started contributing to it. Editor Ina Steiner keeps readers up to speed on all facets of the auction industry. This is the best place to get an objective, critical view of eBay and its changing policies and procedures. There's also a terrific discussion forum where you can discuss eBay freely.

SHIPPING RESOURCES

The Postal Store

shop.usps.gov

It's quite an interesting experience to order something from the post office, pay nothing for it, and, a few weeks later, to have something delivered to your door. Take advantage of this service: go to the store and order some Priority Mail boxes yourself. Once you register, you can use the same ID and password for the Postal Service's Click 'n' Ship service if you need it. You'll find some box sizes you won't be able to pick up at the post office otherwise.

Endicia Internet Postage

www.endicia.com

I have talked to a number of eBay sellers who use this service for printing out postage and mailing labels rather than the U.S. Postal Service. It's a useful alternative to the USPS that comes in handy, particularly if you don't want to pay any more money to them than you have already.

United Parcel Service

www.ups.com

I know many sellers who love UPS and depend on it every week. They particularly like the fact that you can call for a pickup beforehand and the delivery person will come to your business or residence and take your packages away. They've gotten to know their delivery person over the years, too.

OTHER RESOURCES

Craigslist

www.craigslist.org

I realize this is a book full of eBay tips. Nevertheless, eBay isn't the perfect place to sell everything. If you want to get rid of a couch, a big easy chair, or an appliance, turn to the local version of this site that's nearest to you. You can even post photos there. What's more, you don't have to worry about shipping; you can have the buyer pick up from you.

buySAFE

www.buysafe.com

Some of the big-time PowerSellers I've interviewed signed up for buySAFE on a trial basis. I know they were skeptical about the company's claims that their "seal of approval" attracts more bids and higher prices. At least one of those sellers is still using buySAFE. This site verifies that transactions from sellers listed are insured by buySAFE for up to $25,000. If the seller doesn't follow through with the sale and the buyer doesn't get what was ordered, buySAFE will reimburse them. Sellers have to pay one percent of the price of each item sold, submit an application, and provide other financial information.

SpareDollar
www.sparedollar.com
At least two sellers I've talked to use SpareDollar, which they describe as an affordable and useful auction service. SpareDollar only costs a flat rate of $9 per month; for that rate, you get unlimited photo hosting space and all the other services you can use.

Vendio
www.vendio.com
Vendio is a popular service with eBay sellers. It includes a robust online store feature. It's best known for providing users with an animated "filmstrip" of photos that advertise their items for sale.

Infopia
www.infopia.com
Infopia is a terrific option if you want to not only establish an eBay business, but an e-commerce website as well. I know one seller, Shiana.com, that used Infopia to build a successful business selling handmade jewelry to a worldwide audience.

GoDaddy.com

www.godaddy.com

Lots of different domain name registrars are available to help you lock down a name you can use on the Web. This is one I happen to be familiar with because I've used it myself. I chose it because it was far more economical than other registration options.

iOffer.com

www.ioffer.com

I'm not thrilled with the level of customer service on this site, but it does provide you with a good alternative to eBay. You can "port" your unsold items to iOffer using a tool called Mr. Grabber. Then you can put them online for a fixed price or invite offers from interested parties.

eBay Workshops

http://pages.ebay.com/community/workshopcalendar/
current.html

To my mind, eBay's workshops are among the best sources of information when it comes to learning specific aspects of buying or selling on the site. Often, sessions are conducted by eBay sellers themselves. Browse through the archives of past workshop sessions to find a topic that interests you.

Appendix B:

Discussion Groups and Sources of Support

eBay's community areas—places where members gather to exchange greetings and information—are among its most lively resources. After all, everyone needs some help and advice from time to time. This appendix gathers together places, both on eBay and off, where you can gather with other buyers and sellers to trade information and socialize.

ANSWER CENTER

http://pages.ebay.com/community/answercenter/index.html

There are many ways to get answers on how to use a particular eBay feature. You can click a link to Q & A discussion boards about Search, the eBay toolbar, Turbo Lister, feedback, etc.

AOL CAFÉ

http://chatboards.ebay.com/chat.jsp?forum1&
thread12 .

This is the equivalent of the eBay Café for AOL
users who can joke, talk, or make friends.

AUCTIONBYTES

www.auctionbytes.com

There are two newsletters, one that appears twice
a month and a NewsFlash that appears several
times each week. Both are chock-full of tips, news
articles, and suggestions for how to profit on eBay.

AUCTION GUILD

www.auctionguild.com

If you want a counterpoint to what eBay says
about itself, this is a site that keeps track of
every problem that has occurred with eBay.
Some examples include service outages, fraud,
and privacy invasions.

COMMUNITY HELP BOARD

http://pages.ebay.com/community/boards/index.
html

Some of what is here could be called games, but
there are also impromptu opinion polls. Among
other features are actual questions about eBay
pages loading slowly and problems with sellers.

COMMUNITY HUB OVERVIEW
PAGE

http://pages.ebay.com/community/index.html

This is a good place to find discussion groups and
post messages of your own. Click on "Community"

in the eBay navigation bar or go directly to the URL indicated previously. Then click on one of the groups listed under the heading Category-Specific Discussion Groups.

EBAY CAFÉ
http://chatboards.ebay.com/chat.jsp?forum1& thread1
This is where to go to exchange small talk or discuss more serious topics with new and old friends from all over eBay.

EBAY CATEGORY SPECIFIC CHAT ROOMS
http://pages.ebay.com/community/chat/
Sellers can communicate with competitors in their category in specific chat rooms. This is a useful way to compare notes and share ideas about what sells and what doesn't in a chosen area.

EBAY DISCUSSION BOARDS
http://pages.ebay.com/community/boards/index. html
These discussion groups are arranged by category. You can discuss problems, get tips, or meet experienced users in an area of your choice.

EBAY GROUPS—REGIONAL
http://groups.ebay.com/index.jspa
eBay hooks you up with members from all over the world. But sometimes there's no place like home. If you have a concern that relates to your own U.S. state, this is the place to meet other eBay users who live nearby.

EBAY GROUPS—SELLER GROUPS

http://groups.ebay.com/index.jspa?categoryID1

Sellers have their own special niche here. You'll meet all kinds, including PowerSellers and eBay store owners.

EBAY Q & A CHAT ROOM

http://chatboards.ebay.com/chat.jsp?forum1& thread21

Are you a beginner with a question regarding eBay? Other eBay users will do their best to give you guidance and direction at this site.

EBAY MARKETPLACE RESEARCH & SALES REPORTS DISCUSSION BOARD

http://forums.ebay.com/db1/forum.jspa? forumID=1000000020

This board is for eBay members who want to learn and share best practices with other community members about eBay data products available to help sellers track and analyze their sales over time. If you have problems or complaints about the way eBay tracks your sales, this is the place to compare notes with your fellow sellers.

EBAY WORKSHOPS

http://forums.ebay.com/forum.jsp?forum93

Who better to learn from about how to perform a task on eBay than your peers? You'll find postings of online discussions to be held in the future as well as archives of past discussions.

FROOGLE

http://froogle.google.com

Froogle is Google's search tool for current consumer merchandise being sold in online stores. If you are selling new or nearly new electronics, sporting goods, or other items, go here for an accurate survey of the current prices.

INFOPIA

http://www.infopia.com

This software management service can help sellers with various functions. For example, they can design their website and then send Infopia the PDF files (PDF stands for Adobe Acrobat Portable Document Format). Infopia also has software that helps businesses manage inventory and automate tasks like email communications to high bidders and relisting of items. One of Infopia's products, the Configurator, actually allows buyers to customize sales items and create their own sales listings.

IMAGES/HTML BOARD

http://chatboards.ebay.com/chat.jsp?forum1&thread42

If you get stuck on something techie when you're creating your auction listings, help is to be found here. You'll find tips on posting images and formatting with HTML, for example.

USEFUL INFORMATION FOR EBAY

www.drexelantiques.com/ebayhelp.html

Instead of articles or tips, this site has links to virtually any part of eBay's site. Its organization by topic makes it both extensive and practical.

MARKETWORKS

http://www.marketworks.com

Many sellers consider a sales management software service to be their business partner. A few of the services they provide include checking emails, sending end-of-sale acknowledgements to high bidders, and relisting items.

PROFESSIONAL EBAY SELLERS ALLIANCE (PESA)

http://www.gopesa.org

This group of high-volume sellers makes suggestions about how to improve eBay. Members have to meet two of the following criteria: $25,000 in gross sales, $1,500 per month in eBay fees, five hundred feedbacks in the past thirty days, or five hundred listings in the past thirty days.

SELLER CENTRAL DISCUSSION BOARD

http://forums.ebay.com/db2/forum.jspa?forumID143

This board helps eBay members learn selling tips, tools, and resources to maximize sales and building a thriving eBay business. eBay sellers, with the support of eBay staff, share their experiences, their feedback, and their most effective, time-tested strategies for success.

Index

B

M